G

IN THE BATH

RELAXING IN THE
EVERYWHERE PRESENCE OF GOD

STEPHEN MITCHELL

First published by O Books, 2006
An imprint of John Hunt Publishing Ltd.,
The Bothy, Deershot Lodge, Park Lane, Ropley, Hants, SO24 0BE, UK
office@johnhunt-publishing.com
www.o-books.net

USA and Canada
NBN
custserv@nbnbooks.com
Tel: 1 800 462 6420 Fax: 1 800 338 4550

Australia
Brumby Books
sales@brumbybooks.com
Tel: 61 3 9761 5535 Fax: 61 3 9761 7095

Singapore
STP
davidbuckland@tlp.com.sg
Tel: 65 6276 Fax: 65 6276 7119

South Africa
Alternative Books
altbook@global.co.za
Tel: 27 011 792 7730 Fax: 27 011 972 7787

GOD
IN THE BATH

RELAXING IN THE
EVERYWHERE PRESENCE OF GOD

STEPHEN MITCHELL

BOOKS

Winchester, UK
Washington, USA

Stephen Mitchell is so entertaining that you don't at first realise how subtle he is. He's out to change the way we think - and to show that religious thought is still very much alive.

DON CUPITT, EMMANUEL COLLEGE, CAMBRIDGE

This is as a bold and innovative new way of writing anthropology from a theological perspective. Stephen grasps the power of the imagination to give our lives meaning, and now shows how we no longer need to rely on 'given' religious or philosophical truths...this makes a challenging read and I highly commend it to thoughtful Christians, and indeed members of all faiths and none currently struggling for a viable philosophy for 21st century living.

DR DAVID HART, INDIA SECRETARY THIRUVANANTHAPURAM, WORLD CONGRESS OF FAITHS

This book is a welcome breath of fresh air in a world bedevilled by arguments about the nature of faith and belief which quickly reach fever pitch. There is a cutting edge because Stephen challenges radical Christians to rediscover the revolutionary insights within orthodoxy and proclaim them within a world which is being held to ransom by the religious right.

The author takes his readers on a journey of exploration using examples from contemporary culture to illustrate his theme. Belief in God is not about expressing an opinion or even a conviction, it is about re-discovering the "tingle factor" in religion. *God in the Bath* is a refreshing bath and a timely tonic for tired believers.

**THE RIGHT REVD RICHARD LEWIS
BISHOP OF ST EDMUNDSBURY AND IPSWICH**

A bright and engaging restatement of Christian faith for today.

THE RIGHT REVD RICHARD HOLLOWAY, AUTHOR OF DOUBTS AND LOVES

A penetrating, powerful, incisive exploration of what it really means to believe in God. For those despairing of irrational religious hysteria on one side and boring empty churches on the other, Stephen Mitchell in *God in the Bath* offers a viable compelling alternative.

JOHN SHELBY SPONG, AUTHOR OF THE SINS OF SCRIPTURE

This little book is destined to become a spiritual classic. Stephen Mitchell has provided us with a reworking of the Christian faith that makes sense of God in the everyday things of life for ordinary people. If you thought that God was dead, think again and read this wonderfully provocative, yet strangely comforting exploration of the God who is everywhere. The many spiritual pearls of wisdom found in this book connect the Christian journey of faith with the odyssey of life. For those who have been put off by propositional Christianity, this is the perfect antidote. A wonderfully refreshing and invigorating reading of Christianity.

NIGEL LEAVES, AUTHOR OF ODYSSEY AND SURFING ON THE SEA OF FAITH

To Frances and Jennifer

CONTENTS

Chapter 1
in

This book is about a little word: the religious use of the word *in*. There are lots of things people say they believe *in*, from fairies to UFOs, from playing the game, to having a good time. It's a shorthand way of saying these things exist, or that they're good for us, or to be trusted. But when, as Christians, we say that we believe *in* God, it's an almost literal use of the word *in*. We believe *in* God. God is our environment, our world, our life.

This book, then, has its roots in a very traditional understanding of God. In theological jargon, it's about God's omnipresence, God being everywhere. Because God is everywhere, we are, wherever we are, *in* God. So it shouldn't be difficult to believe *in* God. We shouldn't have to struggle to get our heads round impossible questions. We are already *in* God. Belief isn't like taking an exam; it's like taking a bath. We need to learn to relax and let ourselves be revived in God's presence.

But this book is also a radical book. As we look more closely at God's omnipresence and what we find ourselves to be *in*, the implications for our faith are shocking and revolutionary. This book is also about the church. I've been a priest in the Church of England for twenty-five years, a church that is rapidly declining in numbers and influence, and a church that is increasingly dominated by more fundamentalist expressions of faith. I find many people struggle to understand, let alone accept, these literal expressions of Christian faith. Either they give up on them, or else, somewhat sheepishly, they keep their thoughts to themselves. They don't need to. Some of the things they struggle with are a travesty of traditional Christian belief. It is high time radical Christians had the confidence to secure their place right at the heart of the Christian church. Far from being made to feel that their radical faith is a poor relation to real Christianity, radicals need to find their voice and demonstrate the deep roots of their faith.

Over the last twenty years, I have found inspiration to do this within the Sea of Faith Network that I helped to found.[1] It's an organisation that attracts people of different faiths and different Christian denominations, as well as people of no religious faith, atheists, agnostics and humanists. It's an exciting forum. It's also a challenging forum because some in the network would like to see a drastic re-shaping of the Christian faith. They talk about a

"Christianity without God" and a need to re-interpret Christian doctrine.[2] I agree with them; faith has got to change. But it often feels to me as if they have thrown the baby out with the bathwater. I want to say to them that there is, within the radical Christian tradition, an orthodox understanding of God that is startlingly revolutionary and demands its own revolution.

I owe a great debt to members of Sea of Faith and an even greater debt to the people I've ministered to in Leicestershire and Suffolk. Thanks to the Venerable John Cox, Frances Mitchell, John Shield and Patti Whaley who all gave detailed and helpful criticism on early drafts of the manuscript. Above all thanks to my daughters, Frances and Jennifer, and my wife, Lucy, for their constant inspiration and encouragement.

Chapter 2
in the bathroom

A friend showed me an advert for some toiletries. (You know there's something wrong when a best friend shows you an advert for toiletries.) It was an advert for a new brand of lavender toiletry. *Experience four contemporary interpretations of lavender - soul, faith, prayer and spirit.*[1]

put your *faith* in white lavender and vanilla orchid
cleanse your *soul* with alpine lavender and eucalyptus
answer *prayer* with juniper and french lavender
revitalise your *spirit* with asiatic lime and lavender

What on earth has happened to faith today? Faith was once the inheritance of the saints. It inspired martyrs to face death and missionaries to travel the world. What's it doing repackaged as *a deep cleansing clay-based face mask?* The *Spirit*, the power of God, descended like tongues of fire upon the disciples' heads, driving them out to preach the good news.[2] Now it's being marketed as *Spirit* an *exfoliating body scrub gel*. It certainly gives new meaning to total immersion and baptism in the Spirit!

The advertisement goes on to remind us that lavender has been used for its perfume and medicinal properties since Greek and Roman antiquity. Oils and spices have always been used in religious ceremonies. But what is happening to faith when *Prayer*, the deepest communion of the human with the divine, becomes a *foaming body wash*? Do we look forward to washing ourselves with *Blood of the Lamb* soap?

Perhaps faith today needs to ravish the senses more. Perhaps it needs more "tingle factor", something to make the hairs on the back of our neck stand up on end.

> like the precious oil upon the head,
> running down upon the beard,
> upon the beard of Aaron
> running down on the collar of his robes.[3]

Perhaps faith's believers need to be more sensual like the woman of the city who

> brought an alabaster flask of ointment, and standing behind Jesus, began to wet his feet with her tears and wipe them with the hair of her head, and kiss his feet,

and anoint them with the ointment.[4]

Perhaps there should even be more burning of incense; but surely, its gospels shouldn't be reduced to four interpretations of lavender. Has faith today become a touchy-feely spirituality of the bathroom? Go into your room; shut the door; light the candle; turn on the bath taps and pour out your *Soul, the alpine lavender and eucalyptus bath oil.*

One can hear the prophets of doom already preparing faith's lament:

Harken, O ye peoples.
Hear the word of the Lord.
Woe to faith and woe to the people of faith.
Faith has fled into the bathroom,
embarrassed herself and hidden herself away.
She stares at herself in the mirror,
too shy to show her face,
Through her tears she repairs her face in vain.
What can restore her beauty?
How can she hold her head up high in the house where
she was once its head?
No one comforts her.
No one misses her.
She is forgotten
and has forgotten her own name.
Woe to faith and woe to the people of faith.

Has faith retreated to the bathroom?

We can imagine faith downstairs, running from the study, having been overwhelmed and shouted down by science and technology. Once heralded as the Queen of the Sciences, faith struggles to hold her own. Her boast to change the world is ridiculed by industrial and technological revolutions. Faith's miracles are childish conjuring tricks compared to the awesome powers of the atom and the computer chip. Who needs to turn water into wine when the supermarket shelves are stacked high with vintages from every part of the world? Where's the buzz in praying when there's the constant, comforting communication of text messages and e-mails? What has faith to say to a world whose increasing knowledge threatens gridlock on the information superhighway?

We can imagine faith escaping from the kitchen. There, around the table, people are pouring out their troubles. They are worried about their health. They are in pain over their partners and lovers. They struggle to juggle work, home-life and relationships, to make time for themselves, and to create a balance and harmony in their lives. They are fearful for the future and their children. They worry about the world. But they don't listen to faith. They don't heed her advice. Faith's talk about sin only makes them feel worse. There's enough guilt around already without adding to it. They prefer the explanations of the psychiatrist and the psychoanalyst, and the remedies of the doctor, the therapist and the aromatherapist.

Upstairs we can imagine faith fleeing from the bedroom, embarrassed and confused. Once she delighted in Solomon and Vatsyayana. Now there's no *Song of Songs*, no *Kama Sutra*. Faith appears frigid and prudish. The more faith pontificates obsessively about sex, the more out of touch faith appears to be.

Faith is simply no longer the life and soul of the party, sometimes no longer even invited. Once upon a time, faith was the pillar of society. It bound the community together. Through faith people worked together, pulled together and knew their place in the world. Faith told men when to feast and when to fast. Faith told their women when to speak and when to be silent, what to cook and what to wear. Once faith dictated the worlds of art and architecture, music and morals. Once rulers and scientists alike were under faith's control. Not anymore. Now globalized industries, films, fashion and football shape our cultural world. What hope has faith got of competing with Mickey Mouse and MacDonalds, *Titanic* and *Tomb Raiders*, Homer Simpson and Harry Potter?

The story of faith's retreat is like the priest in Joanne Harris' novel *Chocolat*.[5] Into his village comes an irreligious, single mother, Vianne Rocher. She has the audacity to open a *chocolaterie* on the first day of Lent right opposite his church. It's a declaration of war, chocolate versus the church. Day by day villagers give in to temptation and visit the shop-cum-café to taste the heavenly, handcrafted confectionary. Soon their chocolate communion becomes their confessional. Here, in the *chocolaterie*, they share their joys and secret sorrows and find that Vianne brings an absolution and redemption to the village that the church and its priest could never give. Outcasts and sinners find themselves accepted and transformed, and the impotent priest is brought to judgment in his own chocolate hell.

The story of faith's retreat is like the story of the English country parson. Once he ruled the parish. He was the local doctor, the officer of the law and the magistrate, as well as the teacher and preacher. Today the clergy are marginalized from the mainstream of most peoples' lives. Their expertise has been taken over by professionals. Now the English country parson is a figure of fun, a caricature. He's Rowan Atkinson's portrayal of the befuddled, tongue-tied vicar in the film *Four Weddings and a Funeral*, struggling to bless the happy couple "In the name of the Father and of the Son and of the Holy Goat".

As an English parish priest for twenty-five years, this could be my story. Some give my own church, the Church of England, a future of no more than forty years, some as little as twenty. In only ten years, from 1979 to 1989, attendance at churches across all denominations in the UK dropped by 13%. In the following decade from 1989 to 1999, the fall was an even greater 22%. The proportion of people who believe in a God has dropped from 43% in the 1950s to 31% in the 1990s while over the same period, the proportion of Britons espousing atheism has rocketed from

2% to 27%.[6]

CHURCH DEAD & BURIED BY 2040 read the headline of a London daily in response to these statistics. And good riddance, some say. A friend said to me: faith is a fag end, burning itself out and doing incurable harm in the process. How many wars have been fought in the name of faith? How much prejudice, cruelty, indoctrination and immorality goes under the excuse of faith? How much terrorism and martyrdom wreaks havoc in the name of faith?

Matthew Arnold once depicted the retreat of faith in a memorable image. In his poem, "Dover Beach", he likened faith to the sea retreating from the shore as the tide goes out.

> The Sea of Faith
> Was once, too, at the full, and round earth's shore
> Lay like the folds of a bright girdle furl'd.
> But now I only hear
> Its melancholy, long, withdrawing roar,
> Retreating, to the breath
> Of the night-wind, down the vast edges drear
> And naked shingles of the world.[7]

Has faith retreated to the bathroom? Is the "melancholy, long, withdrawing roar" the last gurgle of faith as it disappears down the plug-hole? I don't think so.

Certainly the bathroom has become a retreat, but not an escape. No longer the smallest room in the house, we will sacrifice a bedroom to have our bath and shower *en suite*. The bath stands away from the wall like a baptismal font for full immersion. Candles and incense, soft lighting and perfume, marble and music, elegance and grand design add to the sense of sacred space. Here is a temple to relaxation, meditation and healing. Our showers and jacuzzis pulsate with the waters of new life, revitalizing our spirits. Here we are rediscovering a long-forgotten truth about God.

In the sixth century BCE, a Cretan prophet, called Epimenides, teased the world by declaring that all Cretans are liars; but his *Hymn to Zeus* contains more than a logical paradox.

> The Cretans:
> always liars
> evil beasts
> idle bellies -
> they fashioned a tomb for thee
> O holy and high one
> but thou art not dead
> thou livest and abidest forever
> for in thee we live and move and have our being.[8]

Epimenides was also famous for freeing Athens of a devastating plague. In desperation, the local priests had tried to find a cure for the plague by offering sacrifices to every single one of all the known local gods. Epimenides concluded that as all the known gods had failed them, the cure for the plague must lie in offering worship to an Unknown God.

In Athens, Epimenides found a culture not unlike our own. It was the god-capital of the world. "Never have I seen so many gods," he is reported to have said on his arrival. "It's easier to find a god than a person." He would say the same today, on arrival in one of our major cities, where there are temples for all the major world faiths, and where every kind of spirituality is advertised in newspapers and magazines. And yet, as well as having so many gods and spiritual paths from which to choose, we too find those who have "fashioned a tomb" for God and announced his death.

Many years after Epimenides, St Paul, testifying to Athens, took up the phrase "In thee we live and move and have our being".[9] We should take it to heart too. If God is indeed, like the air we breathe, in and all around us, to find God we should breathe slowly and deeply, letting ourselves be filled with the breath of life. If God is indeed like the waters of the sea in which the fish lives and moves and has its being, then to find our spiritual cure, we should take to the water, and let the water of life flood over us. Our lavish and pleasurable ablutions in the bathroom symbolize a new, spiritual rediscovery of faith in the Unknown God in whom we live and move and have our being.

Chapter 3
in God

"In God we live and move and have our being." Lines from the poem of a sixth century BCE Cretan prophet, testifying to an Unknown God, sound just too pagan, too agnostic and too wishy-washy to have anything to do with Christianity's God. Yet this really is the God of Christian orthodoxy.

To demonstrate this, I want to take as an example what, as Christians, we say about creation. If this seems just a little too theological, think of it as the necessary preparation of running the bath. (And why not go and get a drink while the bath is filling up!)

Christian teaching about creation, on the face of it, sounds very straightforward. Who made the world? God made the world. God made everything. But there is a lot more to say about the Christian doctrine of creation and the end result is mind-boggling. Here are three further things we say about creation.

Firstly, there must be no sense that creation was a one-off event in the past. We don't want to imply that God made the world like a builder building a house, who then goes off, leaving it to be owned and occupied by someone else. Creation is not a past event but an on-going present process. The more ambiguous phrase "maker of heaven and earth", which we use in the Apostles' Creed, gives a better sense of this on going activity.

Secondly, the way God creates is very different from human design. God doesn't have ideas. God has no need to draw up plans. God has no need to get the builders in. God speaks and it is done (except, of course, God doesn't actually speak). What God thinks comes to pass (except, of course, God doesn't actually think). If all our thoughts sprang immediately into action it would be truly chaotic and frightening, not to say embarrassing. But for God, there could be no other way for things to come about. The verb "to make" hardly describes such an extraordinary and mysterious process of coming to be.

Then *thirdly*, God's way of creating is even more extraordinary in that God doesn't need any materials out of which to make the world. In the beginning there is God, not God and some stuff-out-of-which-he-makes-his-creatures. When we make something, we use what is already there. From it we build houses and write books and, with luck, our efforts last for some time. But for Christians there must be no sense of there being anything there before God, or of creation carrying on without God. Without the ever-sustaining presence of God, everything collapses, even the very stuff of creation; for creation is created *out of nothing*. Creation, and all that is, is utterly dependant upon the ever present word of God.

Now if this is what as Christians we say about creation, it is hardly summed up in the phrase "God made the world". If we ask the question "Who made the world?" we look for an answer in the form "*God* made the world" or "*Nobody* made the world", but that is not going to take us to the heart of our Christian teaching about creation. A better question would be "Who makes the world?" This not only has the present, on going sense to it - "Who is making the world?"- it also has the sense of giving something worthwhile to the world - "Who makes the world a good place?" "What makes the world go round?"

But we haven't quite finished. We have yet more to say about creation. *Fourthly*, we want to maintain a clear distinction between God and the world God makes. God and creation, the creator and the created, are separate and distinct. Of course, we make the same kind of distinction between ourselves and anything we make (even though we are both part of creation and basically made out of the same stuff). Sometimes we say "There's a lot of me in this work" but we are clear that there is a difference between what we've made and ourselves.

When it comes to talking about God, God really is

different. God is certainly not just another thing. To say creation is one thing that exists and God another thing that exists would be to put God in the same category as all other existing things. But God, so we say, is not just another thing; God is the source of all things, the creator of all things. God is not just another thing, different to other things; God is completely different, *altogether different.*

One of the ways this has been expressed in Christian teaching is by saying that God is not a being, another being, or even another type of being. God is "beingness itself".[1] We might try and put it another way by saying that God is not a thing, or a different type of thing, but "thinginess itself". More poetically, we might say that God is not alive, like all the things to which God gives life, but "life itself". Or more teasingly, we might say God is not real but "reality itself".

So we must reformulate our question yet again. The question "Who made the world?" did not take us to the heart of Christian teaching about creation. A better question was "Who makes the world?" Now we discover that we need a question that takes us to the mystery of "life itself". What is being? What is reality? What is common to everything that is?

We begin our exploration of the doctrine of creation with a simple, straightforward question, "Who made the world?" It's a question that looks for a straightforward answer. It's a question we can get our teeth into. For a start we can look for evidence that the world has been made. We can examine the intricate patterns and structures of life and wonder at the enormous scale and energies of the universe. We can look at ourselves and the human community, our sense of purpose, our courageous and self sacrificial actions, our appreciation of beauty and our capacity to love. Is all this not evidence of a world designed and purposefully made?

Soon we stumble across other evidence, evidence to suggest a purposeless, uncreated world. We listen to those scientists, psychologists and cosmologists who argue that everything we see around us can be explained from simple, first principles. Even the beauty, the courage and the love come from a built in need to protect ourselves and our species. Is there any need for a creator God?

If we persist with our first, simple question "Who made the world?" and don't immediately find an answer, at least we have plenty to go on and plenty to keep us going. There's evidence to find and lots to argue about, and our search for an answer will take us into all areas and aspects of life. But we rejected that simple, straightforward question. Consequently, all that research becomes irrelevant. Interesting and engaging though it is, all the evidence of design in the universe, all the counter-arguments for a self-explaining and self-serving universe, will not take us to the heart of the Christian doctrine of creation. We are trying to answer the wrong question.

Our God, the God of Christianity, is not a God in time,

who in the past made the world. God makes the world, not only makes the world but sustains the world. Indeed God's relationship to the world is closer to us even than that. The world is utterly dependant upon God for its very existence. For God does not just keep things in existence, God is existence itself. God does not just sustain life; God is life.

So in our exploration of what we say about creation, we have been led away from imagining a super-cosmic creation-builder towards a life-giving environment in which we live and move and have our being. We have been led away from a God who may or may not exist to that which is ever-present. Contemplating the mystery of God leads us to the mystery of life.

The implications of believing in God, the God in whom we live and move and have our being, are revolutionary. There is no search for God, for we are already in God. There is no seeking to know God, for God is so intimate to our life that we know God as well as we know ourselves. Our relationship to God is nothing less than our relationship to reality and life. To give the name God to that in which we live and move and have our being, is to give to life, and the mystery at the heart of all being, supreme importance. It is to declare that nothing, no one thing, in all creation is more worthy of the name.

But how are we talk about God? On the one hand, God is too close to call. On the other, God is the great mystery at the heart of all life. How can anything be said about God? As we have seen through the example of creation, at one level the answer is simple: we tell stories about a God making the world. At another level, we talk about God only with the greatest difficulty; only by saying what God is not, and with great restrictions on the way we use the word God.

But if God is that in which we live and move and have our being then we can also look at, and talk about, life, ourselves, and the various features of our world, and through the exploration of our environment discover something of the reality and presence that is at the heart of being.

Chapter 4
in life

Instinctively, it would seem, we are already thinking and talking in terms of the God of life. In a series of little books, the writer and theologian Don Cupitt has listed and charted the way we use the word "life" in hundreds of everyday phrases to express our strongest convictions and deepest feelings.[1] At one time we would have expressed these convictions by using the word God. Now, according to Cupitt, we prefer the word life.

How are we to live life? To the full. We must make the most of life. How should we look on life? As sacred. We must have a reverence for life. Life is precious; we mustn't let life pass us by for we only live once. If we live and move and have our being in God, the life of all life, then this indeed is how we should live.

The richness and variety of life is stunning. The sheer

exuberance of biological life with its gay abandon and profusion is matched only by the extension of cosmological life in time and space. Human life and culture is no less diverse and awe-inspiring. But there is nothing new in discovering the spice of faith in the variety of life. It is fundamental to a belief in the omnipresent God that all life is sacred. It goes without saying that there is no form of life, no variety of life, no life lived, that is without life. All life is intimately in God, the source, sustainer and the life of life itself. High life, low life, the wasted life and the fullest life, the longest life and the shortest life, are all lived in God, all sacred, all revealing of life itself. It's shocking and it's challenging. When we gaze at the stars and pay homage to our saints, conquer mountain peaks and tend our gardens, it's easy to be thankful and say life is good. But watching the slow disintegration of the mind, the preying of species upon species, and human beings at war with human beings, life seems revolting. Some forms of life simply aren't sexy.

So the first challenge that our Christian spirituality calls for is an acceptance of the whole of life. To say yes to God is to say yes to life. Yet this is a very real stumbling block. All life is in God. Everything lives and moves in God. Everyone has their being in God. Yet how, given the awfulness of life, can we possibly accept the whole of life? How can we, in the words of the communion service, give thanks at all times and in all places? It seems an insurmountable challenge.

Many stories are told that would seem to excuse us from having to accept the whole of life. The Fall is one such story. Once upon a time, everything was indeed very good. But from Adam's disobedience onwards, a curse fell upon us, and upon our world. A cloud now covers the sun. Only the occasional shaft of sunlight lights the life we lead, a life that leads ultimately to death. We are forever cursed. Or so the story goes. But the real fall from grace is these stories. God's omnipresence stands. The unknown God in whom we live and move and have our being is still the God of Christians. A God that has absented himself is not the Christian God. A God that is not present at particular times and in particular places is not the Christian God. A faith that begins by seeing life as a curse rather than a blessing is not Christianity. True Christian discernment does not begin by distinguishing blessing from curse, life from death, the light of life from the darkness of sin. It begins by finding appropriate ways of seeing life that will enable us to recognize that which is ever-present, and thereby, to accept life in all its fullness.

To say 'Yes' to life is neither to treat all life in the same way, nor to accept life with a shrug of the shoulders and a "That's life!" To love life is to find the appropriate way to touch and embrace all of its many forms. To show reverence for life is to show a proper respect for all its power, in all its variety. Mountaineers take the utmost care in preparing to make a climb. They know the dangers they are about to face. They know they are not taking a gentle stroll on the fells. Naturalists and anthropologists show the same caution in approaching different forms of life. They know that some species are deadly dangerous. Why should our respect for life demand any less care or differentiation? Probably because we think that there should be no danger in God, no pain in life; that we should understand life and never lose it. But we live and move and have our being in God, the unknown God. There is no understanding life as a whole. We can never step outside everything to gain a vantage point. The starting point for radical faith is in that darkness. That's where the roots grow. That's where life begins.

Sometimes our embrace of life seems more like a wrestler's hold. We struggle to come terms with life. Sometimes it seems as if we are losing our grip on life and are clinging on by our fingernails. Facing the challenge of accepting and working with the whole of life will be on-going. Saying yes to life will require continuing determination and commitment.

To declare that in which we live and move and have our being to be God, is to declare that we will put all our energy and best efforts into life. Life in all its fullness and variety is to be our God. We could, and do, put a lot of energy into all sorts of things. For some "their God is their belly".[2] Our God is that in which we live and move and have our being. We don't reject any one thing in favor of another, nor reject everything in favor of something beyond all things. We reject no part of life and give of our best to the whole of life. To make any one thing, or any group of things, the subject of our whole life's endeavor would be to make of them an idol. To pass life off without a care would be to express an indifference to God amounting to atheism.

Here, then, is the seemingly impossible challenge of faith: to accept and work with the whole of life with all its many facets. But with this challenge comes a surprising liberation, a liberation from dogma. We began exploring the doctrine of creation with dogmatic statements of how the world came to be, and who made it, but soon found ourselves being led to life and an attitude towards life and the need for a way of life that embraced the whole of life. So it is with all Christian doctrine. Believing in the God in whom we live and move and have our being turns all our doctrine into a way of life and our dogma into wisdom.

It is a surprising liberation because we are so used to faith being presented as a series of dogmatic, credal statements. They are given to us like a checklist for a faith examination. If we fail to tick any of the boxes, doubt is cast on our fitness to be a Christian. But the first disciples were simply followers of Jesus who encouraged others to take the same path. These early Christians regarded themselves as followers of The Way.[3] The church can be very reluctant to let go of dogma. At times it has taken extraordinary steps to keep its leaders and members wedded to its dogma. But there is at the heart of the Christian tradition an orthodoxy that undermines church dogma turning it all into a way of life.

To further emphasize the point, when we recite the creed and declare our faith in God, we use a translation of the Latin phrase *credere in Deum*. There are two other Latin phrases that might have been used in the creeds. One is *credere Deo* that could be translated as "believing God", or "believing what God says". The other phrase, *credere Deum* means "believing that God exists". In English, both these phrases can be translated "believing in God". But neither of these phrases is used in the creeds. The phrase used to express Christian belief in the creeds is *credere in Deum*.[4] Belief in God is not expressing an opinion, or even a conviction, about how the world came to be or any other fact about the world. Nor is belief in God expressing a conviction about who is to be trusted in life. If Christians are to be faithful to the creeds, they will not say that they believe that something called God exists, nor that they trust in something called God. Rather they will say that they will put all their energy and living into an acceptance of the whole of life, into that in which they live and move and have their being. Augustine put it like this:

> What is it therefore to believe in him? It is in believing to love, in believing to delight, in believing to walk towards him, and be incorporated amongst the limbs or members of his body.[5]

It is astonishingly simple and astoundingly difficult. We are alive. Life is fundamental to all that we are. How else to explore God but through life? How else do we pay homage to God but by giving reverence to life? How else to become part of God but by immersing ourselves in life? And yet, can we possibly accept all that life throws at us and accept our ultimate end in death? Our Christian pilgrimage is solely directed towards this aim: putting our energy and effort, both as individuals and as communities, in to the whole of life.

Chapter 5
in luck

There is perhaps no better example of the difficulty of accepting the whole of life, and of the challenge to Christian dogma, than that of luck. Most of us use the expression "good luck". A young relative prepares for exams or an important interview and as likely as not we'll say *Good luck!* Do your best, we'll add. Do yourself justice. But we'll still say *Good luck!* If they like sports, drama or music, before their next performance we'll say *Good luck!* Break a leg! Hope it goes well. Don't be nervous, we add. But we'll still say *Good luck!*

After the event, if it doesn't turn out quite as well as they had hoped, if they fail the exam, fluff the interview, or if the performance is a flop, we'll say *Bad luck!* Never mind. There's always next time. Don't worry; we still love you. *Bad luck!*

But do we really mean it? Do we really believe in luck? Is there a place for Lady Luck? (Yes Luck is said to be a lady - a rather naughty, teasing, frivolous lady. She's wayward, unpredictable and unreliable, unlike her Lord and Master who has everything under control).

In the New Testament, in the Acts of Apostles, there is a curious incident where Jesus' disciples cast lots.[1] Judas, having betrayed Jesus, has killed himself, and the disciples want to appoint someone in his place. There are two candidates, Joseph and Matthias. They seem equally good. How shall the disciples decide between them? They cast lots. Of course, the disciples are not putting their trust in Lady Luck. It isn't that both candidates seem equally good and there's nothing to choose between them. It isn't that they believe it doesn't matter which man they choose and so leave it to chance. No, they pray to God to show them which of the two men they should appoint. It's such a difficult decision they must hand it over to God and God will control the dice.

There is a similar episode in the Old Testament, in the Book of Jonah.[2] Jonah is fleeing from the Lord by sea. There's a storm and the sailors are frightened. They believe that one of the passengers has caused the storm. "Come," they say, "let us cast lots, that we may know on whose account this evil has come upon us." They cast lots, fully believing that the dice will reveal which passenger is causing the trouble.

In the Acts of the Apostles and in the Book of Jonah,

lots are cast when it's a matter of life and death. We throw dice when it doesn't matter, when it doesn't matter who goes first, who gets the job, or when we want a bit of fun. When I'm playing a game and winning, someone will accuse me of cheating. "No praying Vicar," they say. "You're not allowed to pray. That's cheating!" But they're joking. They don't really believe in a God that loads the dice.

For us it's a question of responsibility. Are we to live and make decisions, believing that throwing dice can tell us something about the way we should act? Most parents are very concerned if they catch their children playing with a ouija board, and taking it seriously. We'd treat as a joke, a friend who told us that they were going to toss a coin because they didn't know which woman to marry. Heads it will be Mary, tails Martha. We'd throw up our hands in mock horror. "That's ridiculous," we would say. "You can't make the most important decision of your life tossing a coin. Take responsibility for your actions." And we'd be no more impressed if he said, "Oh but I'm going to pray about it. Show me, Lord, who I should marry. If it be Mary let it be heads. If it be Martha let it be tails." This would be beyond a joke. Would he really say to his beloved (or half-beloved) Mary, "My dear Mary, I tossed a coin today and it came down heads, will you marry me?" Luck or no luck, we have to decide where our responsibilities lie.

But it's more serious than this. A couple has a very sick child. They are desperate to find a cure. They learn about a new treatment being tried in another country. "We must take our child there," they say. "We must do everything in our power to get our child treated. We must spend every hour raising money for the funds we need to finance the trip." Or should they? A moment of doubt creeps in. What about their other children? What effect will this commitment have on them? What if they raise their child's hopes of a cure and it doesn't work? Wouldn't they be better to value the last moments they have with their child?

A youngster believes she has a great talent. There's a pop-idol competition coming up. "This is my chance. I must go for the audition." But the day of the audition coincides with an important exam. "What shall I do? I have a God-given talent that I must use. I will not take the exam," she says.

As in both of these examples, in life, it isn't always at all clear what it's right to do. We'll be able to tell in a few weeks time whether they did the right thing, but not now. If the child recovers and goes on to live a happy, healthy, normal life, we'll say how brave the parents were. They were right. But what if things go wrong? On their trip abroad the plane crashes and the family are killed. What if the treatment doesn't work or the family fall apart under the strain? They'd have been better to stay at home, we'll say.

The youngster's pop audition is a success. Rising up the charts she soon becomes one of our best-loved entertainers. On every chat show she urges us to follow her example: "Take your chance, follow your heart, believe in your talent." But suppose on her way to the audition, she trips up the stairs and loses her chance to perform. Or less dramatically, she fails to impress the panel, and having failed to sit the exam, loses her place at college and ends up wasting her life.

In telling such tales, we use the language of luck. We take our *chance*. *Fortunately* things turn out all right. With a stroke of *luck*, the situation is turned round. And we are right to use the language of luck. For how things turn out depends, to some extent, upon luck. Whether we did the best thing sometimes depends upon how things turn out. And how things turn out is sometimes a matter of luck.

A new dimension is added to our stories when we recognize the element of luck in them. We commend the Good Samaritan for his actions in helping the roadside victim of a robbery.[3] We condemn the priest and Levite who "passed by on the other side." But it's not quite so simple. We ought to recognize the element of luck in the story. The Samaritan might have stopped, gone over to the man and been attacked himself. Did he know the robbers had gone? And what would his wife and family say to that? Why was he so foolish as to go blundering in? At least the priest and the Levite not only reported the incident to the Jerusalem police (they might have done!), they also fulfilled their obligations to the temple and prayed for the injured man (again, they might have done). The oil the Samaritan was carrying, and poured onto the victim's wounds, might have gone rancid. The Samaritan might have lifted the man onto his donkey and because of the man's injuries done incurable damage to his back. Did he really know so much about first aid? Did he undertake a risk assessment of the situation first?[4] Many of our decisions are taken without knowing what we'd be best doing. There may not be a right course of action. The possibility of tragedy haunts all our decisions. We do what we honestly think is best, recognizing that how things turn out will tell us whether we were right or not. Time will tell, as we say. And in that time, luck may play a big part.

If we don't use the language of luck, we can sound very self-righteous. I made the right decision. Aren't I clever? But our friends quickly bring us down to earth. As it turns out, perhaps you did make the right decision, but things might have been very different. If we don't use the language of luck, we can sound intolerably self-effacing. I failed miserably. I did the wrong thing. I was foolish. But again our friends come to the rescue. Well yes, you were foolish, as it turns out. Had you known what was to happen, you would have been better doing something else. With a bit of luck things might have been very different. Don't be too hard on yourself.

It may seem very reasonable to use the language of luck but there are Christians who say that all things happen according to God's will. Life is so complicated that we simply cannot know everything that is going to affect our decisions. But God knows, they say. Our actions can so easily have tragic, unforeseen consequences. But God sees, and nothing happens without his divine governance. His plan for each of us will be fulfilled. But such talk about God gets in a complete mess. Awful things happen in the world, to our friends and ourselves and very often it's someone's fault or something is to blame. But not always. Some things are marvelous. We are happy and healthy, often the result of our hard work, generosity and the actions of others. But not always. Here I am today, born in a relatively peaceful, affluent part of the world. I'm reasonably healthy. What luck! There are many places I might have been born. There are any numbers of diseases that I might have caught. I could say I was blessed and that life has been good to me. But if I said God has blessed *me* with a happy life, meaning that I had been *intentionally* blessed, that would be utterly offensive. The implication is that God has not blessed *him* or *her*. Poor, miserable creatures, God has cursed them with an *un*happy life.

It is no less offensive to say "God has sent this to test you". In many cases the justifiable reply is "I think this test is a little unfair." Sometimes suffering is the result of our stupidity or the actions of others. But some of it is sheer bad luck. And it's better to say so.

This will be a huge challenge to some people's faith. Job, in the Old Testament, suffers great hardship - lightening strikes his sheep and his shepherds, raiders attack and steal his camels, his servants are murdered, his home and his eldest son are swept away in a storm blowing in from the desert. And as if that wasn't enough, he finds himself covered from head to foot in sores.[5] But Job will say nothing against God. He refuses to curse God. And we are taught to admire his fortitude. But in the story, Job suffers all this with the full knowledge and approval of God. Such a test seems to us utterly immoral. In the end, Job's well-being is restored; he lives to a great age and sees his grandchildren and great grandchildren. Not so his servants, or his elder son, who perish as though they were worth no more than his cattle. If this was just a tale of bad luck, we could simply admire Job's patience. But it isn't. And we must also revolt against a God who authorizes such events.

It seems we can hardly avoid talking about luck in all aspects of our life. Even the words "happen" and "happy" have as their root "hap" meaning chance. It seems to present a huge challenge to faith. What becomes of the idea of God the cause of all things, God in control of all things? Can God's providence be providential?

But Christians have always been careful to say that God's blessings are totally undeserved. They are pure unmerited gifts, showered on the just and unjust alike. "God makes his sun rise on the evil and the good, and sends rain on the just and the unjust."[6] Equally misfortune is not to be seen as punishment. "Who sinned," Jesus is asked, "this blind man or his parents?" "Neither," says Jesus.[7]

In traditional Christian teaching, God is not a predictable force in the world subject to a given order. Nor does God control the world like a puppeteer pulling the strings of his puppets. God does not operate the world like a machine operator. Nor can God's followers acquire his blessing as from a drinks dispensing machine. As God's creativity is unlike any human making, so is God's relationship to events in life.

The mystery of God and the mystery of life deepen and extend to the mystery of the tragic, taking the limits of talk about God to extremes. But for Christians who believe that in God they live and move and have their being, such a discipline upon their language is a sign of their resolve to accept, and work with and through, all experiences of life. The predictable and the surprising, the determined and the indeterminate, the ordered and the chaotic, the reasonable and the absurd, the merited and the unmerited, the lucky and the unlucky, are all part of life and all to be painted into the picture of God. Such a discipline also reflects a determination not to distort the true character of life but to recognize and accept all its risky and tragic possibilities.

Those who would live life to the full, who would seek to understand that in which they live and move and have their being, who would seek to know God, seek ways to embrace the whole of life without distorting its true character.

Chapter 6
in Christ

By now, there may well be some intense irritation with our emphasis upon God's omnipresence and with talk of God that is so severely restricted. Surely we have started in the wrong place. As Christians, we don't begin with the God in whom we live and move and have our being and certainly not with an unknown God. Christians begin with the God of Jesus. The unknown God becomes fully known in Jesus. We are first and foremost in Christ.

Certainly, as Christians, we take our name from Jesus Christ; Jesus the Christ. But Christ is the title of an office, a little like Monarch or Prime Minister. Jesus is the Christ, the Messiah.

Jesus, on the other hand, is the name of an individual. So calling ourselves Christians after the office rather than the name, is a little like calling ourselves monarchists rather than Elizabethans. It is true that as often as not Jesus Christ is used simply as a name - a first and last name - but there is a great deal more to the use of the title Christ.

The phrase "in Christ" is one coined by Paul in his letters as part of his creative, theological writing, and has come to express the hopes and beliefs of all Christians. It has no parallel in other writings of the time. In his letters to the churches, Paul addresses the brothers and the saints "in Christ".[1] When we are baptized as Christians, he writes, we are baptized into Christ.[2] We are in Christ. In Christ there is a new creation.[3] In Christ all shall be made alive.[4] Indeed to live is Christ, says Paul in his letters, because "Christ lives in me".[5] In Christ there is neither Jew nor Greek, there is neither slave nor free, neither male nor female but all are one in Christ.[6] Indeed Christ is all and in all, for we are the body of Christ.[7]

Being in Christ is about being truly alive. Being in Christ is being renewed, regenerated and experiencing new life. To be in Christ is to come together in unity, working together and working with differences. To be in Christ is to be fully human and to live in solidarity with the rest of humanity.

We begin our Christian life and relationship to Christ through our involvement with other Christians. It's through the community of Christians that we hear the gospel of Christ. Our spiritual life begins in Christ. For many people, however, the way to Christ is thought to be through a study of Jesus. Researching the gospels they hope to discover everything about the history of the man Jesus and his teaching. From their study, they hope to be in a position to assess his life and form their own judgment as to whether he is indeed the Christ. They move from the history of the man to a confession of his office. Discovering everything about a man who lived 2000 years ago is not that easy but that's not their only difficulty. Even if they are confident that they have a secure knowledge of Jesus' history, they are likely to encounter the difficulty of reconciling the humanity of the man with the divine calling of the office. How can a human being have a calling to be divine?

Traditionally, however, as Christians we move in the opposite direction. We begin in Christ. It is only through being in Christ, within the community of Christians, that there is any witness to Jesus. The gospels were written within and for Christian communities. Unlike a modern historical biography, the gospels were written through the affirmation of Christian churches, perhaps even as a series of readings for their services.[8] So we begin our Christian journey in the company of those who call themselves Christians, in Christ.

This was the starting point for writers in the early centuries of the church and they struggled to give full weight to Jesus' humanity. Some were branded as heretics because they failed to proclaim Jesus a complete human being. Docetists, for example, argued that God only *appeared* to become human in Jesus and was acting out the part of a human being. As God, he certainly could not suffer on the cross. In their attempts to give full weight to Jesus' humanity and combat such heretical views, early Christian writers used the story of Jesus being born of a virgin as evidence for his being truly human. Today, those who use this story do so to proclaim his divinity. For much of Christian history, the work of theologians was seen not as convincing Christians to accept that a human being could have a divine role, but that a divine being should be able to become fully human.

As those who see ourselves as being in God, beginning their journey of faith in Christ as members of the body of Christ, the work of our faith will also be the acceptance of our humanity. In this we follow the example of Christ himself in the Christian story. In the shorthand of the Christmas hymn *Once in Royal David's City*; "He came down to earth from heaven". That's our journey too. Paul writing to the church at Philippi, perhaps quoting an earlier Christian hymn, puts it rather more fully:

> Let your bearing towards one another arise out of your life in Christ Jesus. For the divine nature was his from the first; yet he did not think to snatch at equality with God, but made himself nothing, assuming the nature of a slave. Bearing the human likeness, revealed in human shape, he humbled himself, and in obedience accepted even death death on a cross.[9]

It may seem a remarkable claim that as Christians we

are following Christ from heaven to earth, from a divine life to a human life, from life to death. We usually think of the spiritual journey as running in the opposite direction, from earth to heaven. But our journey is in Christ, and therefore into a deep acceptance of the human condition, even to the point of death.

Now, of course, we already see ourselves as very much coming from the earth. Today we know so much more about our origins and our evolution. We know ourselves to be human beings, a little higher than the apes. But actually most of us are fortunate to begin life in a very protected and pampered environment. As tiny babies, everything is done for us and all our needs are met. We look to our parents to give us everything we could possibly want. We are treated like gods by gods. Even when we are a little older, we probably look upon those around us - our parents and teachers - as being able to do anything and everything for us. Our need is to come down to earth, recognizing our own and our parents humanity as we take responsibility upon ourselves.

We are born into an incredibly technological environment. We can fly from one end of the world to the other. We have supreme confidence that we can discover an amazing amount about our world and even worlds far out in space. The amount of information we have at our fingertips, through the World Wide Web, is mind-numbing. There is something awesomely godlike about it. We watch events as they unfold. News channels broadcast wars and disasters as they happen. To see everything going on in the world, knowing about everything in our world, and in communication with everything in our world, is to be in the position of the gods. We often describe people who are being dictatorial as 'playing God', but we all play God. Yet there are severe limitations to human knowledge and power. Human life is vulnerable and fragile, and at risk of the tragic. Our spiritual journey must be a journey into our humanity, into a real acceptance and recognition of the limitations of being human. For us, with Christ, our journey is down to earth.

There are some tell tale signs of our failure to make this journey and to accept our humanity. One is our attitude towards our environment. Gods and heavenly beings don't depend upon an environment. They create new worlds for their creatures to live in. Indeed because Gods are spiritual beings, without bodies, they don't need any kind of environment to sustain them. But we do. Like every other animal, we need an environment to survive. Human beings are utterly dependant upon the world they live in. And a society that doesn't look after its environment must be a society that shows signs of a lack of spiritual well being. The way we have stripped parts of the world of resources, and pumped pollutants into the atmosphere and onto the land, is a sign of our failure to recognize that we are utterly dependant, as human beings, upon a sustainable environment. If we destroy our environment, we not only destroy the habitat of many creatures, we destroy ourselves. For we are an integral part of that environment and to live as though we were not is to live as though we were God.

Another sign of a reluctance to come down to earth and accept our humanity is an inability to accept growing old. The adverts show us a fantasy of people, ever young, ever fit and ever healthy. Not that there is anything at all wrong in being young, fit and healthy. But to be human is to grow old, it's to lose our abilities and show signs of aging. And failure to accept the aging process, whether by those who are growing old or by those who are young, must be a sign of a society's lack of spiritual health. The same could be said for those for whom we devise all sorts of politically correct words; the differently-abled, those from particular ethnic and social groupings, the vertically and chronologically-challenged. Human beings are different with different abilities. The perfect human being is not the young fit, beautiful icon with a massive IQ. Being human is to accept that we come in all shapes and sizes and with many different abilities.

A further sign of our failure to come down to earth is the low self-esteem of so many people in society. The contrast between our imagined, God-like knowledge and powers and the frailty and vulnerability of human life produces expectations impossible to fulfill. Life can be utterly horrid and painful. That is hard enough to accept, but added to this pain and sorrow, there is the feeling that it just doesn't seem fair. It seems so utterly unfair at times.

And yet when, or if, we are able to stand back, we know that this is simply what it is to be human. We know and accept that nature is red in tooth and claw; that life can be hard, miserable and tragic. To be human is to be part of that life. We are not gods and should therefore have no expectation of a life lived on fluffy clouds in everlasting sunshine. It doesn't make life any easier to accept. It doesn't make life seem any less of a cruel joke at times. It doesn't make the senselessness of suffering seem any more meaningful. But deluding ourselves that we are anything but human, and somehow have a right to anything but a human life, cannot but add to our pain and undermine our self-esteem.

We call ourselves Christians because we try to follow Christ. Remarkably that isn't following a path from down here on earth up to the heavenly heights. It isn't a process of becoming more and more godlike. Over and again the Gospel writers impress us with their emphasis upon Jesus' humility. He rides into Jerusalem on a donkey[10] and washes his disciples feet.[11] His seeks to empower people in their human vulnerability and frailty: those who are ill and bereaved and those who are outcasts from society. To follow the one who was called Son of God is to have the humility to become more and more human, accepting more and more our vulnerability to life and the processes of life that lead to our death. In God our journey into life is deepened through our journey in Christ into our humanity.

Chapter 7
in person

The title Son of God, given to Jesus in the gospels[1] would seem to challenge and undermine our assertion that we our following Christ deeper into our humanity. Here, too, any claims to be liberated from dogma would seem to come unstuck. Aren't the claims for Jesus the most dogmatic of all doctrines? Don't Christians claim for Jesus a co-equality with God, God of God, of one substance with the Father?[2] These claims center on the idea that Jesus is the second person of the Godhead and that in the person Jesus, the divine and the human come together. Now while we may feel the real mystery here lies in what it is to be God, what it is to be a person is no more straightforward.

It is probably lying back, relaxing in the bath that we are most aware of our developing bodies. Here we appreciate their changing shape. Here we love or loathe our inherited features, the cuts and bruises, the wounds and scars, the beauty and disfigurements acquired along our journey through life. Whatever else we are, we are our bodies.

But then we step out of the bath and glance in the mirror. By accident or design, changes to our body can be drastic. Perhaps this is our first tentative glance in the mirror since the accident or the surgery. Perhaps we don't recognize the figure before us. But even if the changes disguise us from our friends, we know it's us. It's still me. I'm the same person. And we know because we remember. We remember being in the bath, being wheeled down the corridor to the operating theatre, the anxiety, the cruel comments made about our appearance. We remember who we were and what happened to us. Perhaps we feel different, very different. This is the new me. My whole outlook has changed. But still we remember. Indeed, in such cases, we almost literally remember. Like taking dry bones and re-clothing ourselves in new flesh, we re-member ourselves.

But we can't laze around in the bath all day and waste time gazing at ourselves in the mirror! We have work to do, a house to run, a family to keep, children to pick up from school. That's what I am, a taxi service, an unpaid hotelier! Family, work and responsibilities all give us a place and a role. At least that's how other people see us. That's how they sum us up, usually in a few seconds. Immediately we're classified, stereotyped and put in our place. They've weighed us up and got the measure of us. Or so they think. Perhaps the role, by accident or design, has been forced upon us. We've been put upon. We're no longer able to be ourselves.

The complexity of what it is to be a person comes home to us in so many ways. When we are unwell, depressed or under medication, we complain that we are not feeling ourselves today. But just who do we feel like? We take up a new job, move into a new situation, or adopt a new role, and we feel that we've found our true selves at last. But then who were we before?

The reality TV show makes fools of the humiliated residents of the *Big Brother* house. But we're not fooled. We sympathize because we are too shrewd not to notice the manipulations of *Big Brother*. They are being used and abused. It's not really them. But then they did agree to become participants. They wanted the prize money and the celebrity status. We know they are playing to the hidden cameras they pretend not to notice. It's all an act of self-promotion. Of course its really them. Our sympathy drains away.

Science-fiction scenarios seem only just over the horizon. Human cloning, brain transplants, and thinking computers, make us wonder - not only what kind of TV shows they'd make - but also just what it is that gives us our identity and makes us human. And so too does the very reality of the losing of our minds and the finality of death.

Whatever we are, we are rooted in our animal past and our genetic inheritance; but we are not just our bodies, and we refuse to allow our physical make-up to determine who we are. We are rooted in all the things that have happened to us, and what we remember of them; but we are not just our histories and we will not allow our experiences to determine who we are. We are rooted in our time, our society and our culture, but we are more than the products of our age. We are all these things; but none of them, will determine who we are. We demand a freedom and a self-determination to be who we want to be, now, here, in the face of the fragility of our world, our personality, our body, memory, mind and the nearness of death. "Remember me, when I'm gone," we cry. "Remember *me*." Our eulogies speak of achievements, relationships and personal characteristics, our biographies tell of upbringing and influences, background and education. We become the story of our lives.

"Remember me, when I'm gone." But what's going? When we appeared, in person, what appeared and in what did it appear? How did that presence relate to the world in which it appeared? And who is the author of the story of our lives?

These questions should remind us of the questions we asked about God. When we say we are in God, what is it that we are in? What is always present to us? Of course, we sometimes talk about forgetting ourselves, being out of our minds, and losing ourselves. Indeed the Gospel demand is to deny ourselves, to lose ourselves to find ourselves. But just how do I deny myself? How can I lose myself?

The very oddity of the demand is disguised by the fact that we use the two words, "I" and "myself" as if they were different. But, of course, I am myself (or I am most of the time). Perhaps we can try to get rid of the difference. How could little old me lose me? It sounds like trying to get rid of my shadow. It's always there. Where can I go to lose myself? If I go down to the shops I am there. If I go to the ends of the earth, I am there. Again we notice the parallel with our talk about God. "Where can I go then from your spirit?" says the Psalmist, "or where can I flee from your presence? If I climb up to heaven, you are there; if I make the grave my bed, you are there also."[3]

Our exploration of ourselves as persons runs parallel to our exploration of the person of God. Our life is in cohabitation with God. So wrote Augustine, "O God, if I know myself I shall know thee".[4] The mystery of God and the mystery of personhood coincide.

With regard to ourselves, as persons, our answers to these questions would, at one time, have been in terms of some spiritual entity of the soul or activity of the mind. We die and the soul leaves the body; the mind loses consciousness. These answers pointed to some kind of stuff out of which our essential personality was thought to be made: spiritual stuff, the stuff of the mind's thinking and ideas. It gave very solid hopes to understanding ourselves and our future. Spiritual stuff had its own heavenly home in which to continue to exist, the stuff of the mind, its own ideal world. But this stuff-ness has lost its appeal. We are not just spirits or ghosts that haunt our bodies, nor are we just presences in our worlds, nor an idea whose time has come. Cut us and we bleed.

And here too we notice parallels with our exploration of the way of Christ, the journey from a heavenly existence into the flesh and blood vulnerability of earthly life. So too, the way to ourselves is the way from disembodied thoughts of spirit and mind to flesh and blood relationships lived out in the world.

For those who see their true selves as being contained in a spiritual, immaterial and eternal soul, their pilgrimage through life will be to preserve their soul. They will avoid anything that might contaminate their soul. They will be forever looking to withdraw from the life of the world into a more secure spiritual home. Their bodies and the life of the world, with its changing culture and fashions, will be but a temporary home soon to be cast aside. They will always be discontented with their bodies and the change and decay of life. They will seek to find themselves within themselves. But those who see the mystery of personhood emerging from the body, the experiences of life, relationships, roles and citizenship, will be drawn ever deeper into those relationships and their well-being. They will seek to find themselves in the work of enriching those relationships in life.

Christian teaching unites the mystery of God and the

mystery of personhood through the mystery of Christ. As Christians we address God in person not because we know of personal qualities that can be attributed to God. God remains the unknown God. Nor is God addressed in person because the mystery of personhood is any better understood. God is addressed in person because our relationship to life is in person.

The Christian relationship to life is therefore considerably deepened. In God, the God in whom we live and move and have our being, we are challenged to accept life in all its fullness because God is the life of all life. Our respect for life turns into a reverence for life. But now we are challenged to see in life the discovery of personhood and the mystery of ourselves. Our reverence for life turns into a love of life.

Chapter 8
in love

Dirt seems to be the latest fascination on British television. Programmes like *How clean is your house?* and *A life of grime* relish the squalor of people's lives and marvel at those who clean up the mess. We are given a tour of cluttered living rooms, kitchens stacked with unwashed dishes and bathrooms too revolting to talk about. How, we wonder, can people live like this, immersed in their own filth. But to our discomfort, environmental health officers uncover the grime just below the surface of all our lives, in the sewers and on the streets.

For our health, safety and well-being we learn what to keep and what to throw away, what is clean and what is dirty. Throw it away, we're told, it's rubbish. Don't touch that! It's dirty! Yuk! Get rid of it.

We may manage to have our refuse taken out of sight

but it's not long before it's back in mind. One way or another, whether for our well-being, health or safety, we soon learn a different attitude to waste. "Where's there's muck, there's brass," as they say in Yorkshire. Waste is profitable: there's money to be made, at the car boot sale and the auction room, at the reclamation yard and the recycling plant. Waste is informative: yesterday's waste is a mine of information to the archeologist, as is human waste to the doctor. Waste is political: we don't want the landfill site and the nuclear storage dump in our backyard. Waste is a serious business.

For the headline writers, it's a small step from a life of grime to a life of crime. The phrases roll out: the dregs of society, the scum of the earth, they are trash, dirt, filth. Take them away. Lock the door. Throw away the key. But they too come back to haunt us and teach us new attitudes. If prisons are not to be over-crowded schools for criminals, there has to be re-training and rehabilitation. Whatever revulsion we feel, however alien it appears, the life we discard has to be embraced and understood.

Our need to segregate is strong. It's how we learn. It's how we make our world. Light and dark, animal and human, male and female, me and you, us and them, life and death, animate and inanimate, sacred and secular - the categorizations are endless. The dividing lines cross and re-cross our world. The dissections become ever more precise and our understanding and knowledge grows. We just can't help it. And we just can't help making value judgments. After all, we make such divisions not only for our own understanding but for our self-preservation as well. So the divisions are clarified and the boundaries strengthened with judgments, rituals and taboos. Soon we have segregated good and evil, right and wrong, the sacred and the profane.

Yet the boundaries have to be crossed and we look with some apprehension on those who do: the refuse collector, the rat catcher, the sewage worker, the pathologist, the prison officer, the funeral director. The fascination they have for their work and the pleasure and satisfaction they derive from it, are met with astonishment. But for those of us who believe in the God in whom we live and move and have our being, the life of all life, the omnipresent God, such people are people of faith and they point us to an understanding of what it is to love God.

St Augustine once asked the question, "What do I love when I love you, my God?"[1] It's not the sort of question to put to your wife, husband or lover! "What do I love when I love you, my dear?" But the oddity of the question comes from the unique understanding of God in traditional belief, from our understanding of God as omnipresent.

If the person I love is in London then they aren't in Zurich. But God, the omnipresent God, is in London and Zurich and Paris and Perth. Indeed wherever there is life and breath, wherever things are real and existing, God is. Whatever the life, be it rapturous or revolting, there is the life of God. And therefore to love God is not to love one person rather than another, one thing rather than another. To love God is to love everyone and everything. To love God is to cross the boundary between the acceptable and the unacceptable.[2]

The point is firmly established within our Christian tradition. It would be normal for me to talk about loving one person but not another. I might say I love Sam but not Fred. Our faith, however, does not allow me to say I love God but I don't love Fred. "If anyone says 'I love God' and hates his brother, he is a liar; for one who does not love his brother whom he has seen cannot love God whom he has not seen."[3] The command is to love God, our neighbor and ourselves. And that is because God is not an invisible Fred, someone we could love in addition to loving Sam, or love as opposed to not loving Fred. Even if the person is unlovable, hateful, vengeful or despicable, if we love God, they are to be loved. That is what it is to love God. That is the way the words are used in our Christian tradition.

Again we are faced with the radical challenge of our Christian faith. The believer isn't asked to *believe* six impossible things before breakfast but to *love* the impossible. This ought to come as no surprise. If God is that in which we live and move and have our being, if God is that which gives life to all life, that which is common to all that is, then exploring, understanding and knowing God will be an exploration of all that is. Saying yes to God will be saying yes to all life. Loving God will be an embracing of all life. The miracle of faith happens when we discover the love that enables us to embraces all things, even those things that are against us, and which brings together even those things that are most sharply divided.

This impossible love, that characterizes the Christian life, has its own word in the Greek New Testament, *agape* (pronounced a-gap-ay) translated in the King James Bible as "charity". It's a word that is not used to any great extent outside the Bible. The Greek word *philo*, which is also used in the New Testament for love, is more widely used in other literature. On the whole *philo* expresses the love of friendship and the love that can exist between members of a family. It is a love that is inspired by, and responds to, the attractiveness of its object. *Agape*, by contrast, is an unconditional love that does not depend on the attractiveness of its object. So Jesus can command his followers to love their enemies and to love indiscriminately. Such love is characterized by forgiveness, by seeking out the lost and by Jesus' own actions in the Gospels of accepting those rejected by society. A woman turns the house upside down looking for the coin she has lost.[4] The father stands day after day looking for the return of his lost son.[5] So Jesus depicts his own ministry as saving the lost, the outcast, the untouchables and the sinners.

We are faced with the mystery of love when, indeed, we do find ourselves able to embrace that which seemed to us unlovable. It may grow slowly, over a long period of time and through much anguish and heart-searching. The work of reconciling ourselves to other people can suffer many setbacks. Forgiving ourselves and those who harm us can be hard. But that it happens, and can deepen into love, testifies to the deepest mystery of human life.

Because this impossible love goes against the grain and requires a complete change of heart, we call it the love of God. It's a deliberately ambiguous phrase. The love of God is what it is to love God, the answer to Augustine's question as to what it is I love when I love God. To love God is to love everything that has the breath of life, even that which is rejected by us and revolts us. But such an impossible love comes, and can come, only from God. So the love of God is the love of God in us. It is God's love, the gift of God, the God of love. The mystery of love and the mystery of God coincide.

The effect of *agape* is transforming. It dispels fear: "Perfect love casts out fear."[6] The same point emerges from the language of "fearing God" in the Christian tradition. When we speak of God protecting us, we are not saying that there is someone who is stronger than any possible threat. Harry is rather big and nasty and I might be very afraid of Harry. When Charlie comes along and says he will protect me from Harry, I feel safe because Charlie is so much bigger and stronger than Harry. Now, however, I shall have to keep on the right side of Charlie because he is so much more powerful. If Charlie turned against me, I would be in real trouble. My fear of Charlie is even greater than my fear of Harry. When in the New Testament, Jesus says, "Do not fear those who kill the body but cannot kill the soul. Fear rather him who can destroy both soul and body in Gehenna,"[7] we are not being asked to look upon God as an even more powerful person than Charlie. If this were the case, then I should end up being even more afraid. I would be afraid of all the terrible things that God could do to me unless I kept on the right side of him. But Jesus goes on to say

Are not two sparrows sold for a penny? And not one of them will fall to the ground without your Father's will. But even the hairs of your head are all numbered. Fear not therefore.[8]

Christian talk about fearing God is not inviting us to fear somebody who is overwhelmingly powerful and can hurt us more than any person we know, it is encouraging us to fear nobody. Jesus does not say "Don't fear these people. Fear someone else instead." Jesus says, "Fear no one".

When everything seems to be against us, and we find ourselves in the most fearful situation, and we discover the peace, resolve and courage to carry on, then once again we come up against the impossibility of love. Faith does not demand that we believe six impossible things before breakfast but that where all else has failed, where we have every reason to give up, we still maintain a courage and an affirming attitude to life.

This is why Christians talk of the death of Jesus as the demonstration of the love of God. According to the Gospel accounts, when all had failed, when all his followers had deserted him, when he was taken outside the city walls to the garbage dump and crucified, Jesus was still forgiving, still life affirming. For the Jews at the time, a hanged man was cursed. There could be no more despicable object; no one could be further from God. And yet it is here, in the embracing of that which would appear furthest from the love of God that the love of God is most clearly seen.

Chapter 9
in spirit

It takes imagination to create something profitable, or even beautiful, from our discarded waste. But people do. And not only professional sculptors. Our children are probably better at it than we are. Give them some cardboard boxes and a few other bits and pieces and they will soon be playing happily, guiding their atomic-fuelled, egg-box spacecraft to the stars.

Imagination is not easy to define. The word would seem to have something to do with images. And when we talk about *the* imagination, we seem to be talking of a rather mysterious faculty that somehow enables us to conjure up fantastic images. On this view, it's perhaps not surprising that in some religious circles imagination gets a bad press. Imagination is fantasy rather than fact, escapism rather than realism. We are lured into following the "imagination of our hearts" rather than the call of duty. At best imagination is to be treated warily, left to the play of artists. At worst, it leads to the creation of false images and idols that seduce us away from truth, reason and God.

But imagination is a more complex range of processes and isn't only to do with art, fantasy and play. It takes imagination to understand the world, to make connections and see underlying patterns in its complexity. We need imagination if we are to make sense of seemingly unrelated events. "Use your imagination", we tell people and indeed, to discover the truth requires us to use our imagination. It takes a leap of imagination to make a scientific discovery just as much as it does to make a sci-fi movie. It takes imagination to act in the world and to have a vision and set goals. To imagine ourselves, or our business, in five years' time is to take the first steps towards developing a program that will further our aims in a realistic and structured way.

Imagination helps us to understand people, empathize with them, and show them compassion. It's one of the driving forces of morality. To follow the Golden Rule, to do to others as we would have them do to us, involves imagining what it would be like to be on the receiving end of our behavior towards others. To be driven to respond to another's needs, we have to imagine what it would be like to be in their shoes. With imagination, the person who comes from a totally different way of life can be seen, despite the differences, as one of us. To ensure that our help is practical, we imagine the various possibilities open to us and their likely effect. We recreate past solutions, to see what we can learn from them and what mistakes we might avoid. To be the sort of people we would like to be, we examine the images we have of ourselves, self-images we largely take for granted and yet which shape our character and responses.

Using our imagination is an essential part of what it is to be a living, thinking, understanding and responsive person. It deepens our insight, clarifies our vision and motivates our action. It's creative, it's liberating and it's key to the exploration of our innermost desires. Imagination is not something that we do in odd moments. It's not reserved for daydreams or art projects. Imagination is absolutely central to every moment of our lives. If we stopped imagining, our world would dissolve into a chaos of shapes and colors and noises.

For the Christian, much of all this work of the imagination is characteristic of the work of the Holy Spirit.[1] In *Genesis*, the creativity of God is seen in the spirit brooding over the face of the waters.[2] In the Old and New Testament it is the spirit that gives wisdom and understanding.[3] Through the spirit prophets have visions and the people dream dreams.[4] In the New Testament, to be filled with the spirit is to give birth to love, joy, peace, kindness and goodness.[5] To live in the spirit is to be bound together in love.[6] In short, we are the image of the creator God. Life in the Spirit is life in the "imagination of God".[7]

This teasing phrase of John Macintyre's seems to claim almost too much: that imagination can take us to the heart of God. Christians are happy to use their imaginations in praise of God, to write music for worship and to create art to adorn their churches and chapels. Being creative is very much seen as reflecting the image of the creative God in us. But more is claimed here. Just as we might talk of the love of God, and say that love takes us to the heart of God, and that to be in love is to be in God, so to be in imagination is to be in God. Imagination and imagining take us into God.

It's a radical claim that seems to put God into the realm of fantasy and unreality. But we need to remind ourselves that imagination is not only seen in art and play, in fantasy and dreams. It's so easy to forget that even the most abstract scientific papers are written in images and metaphors. Anatomy provides a striking example. For most of us, the closest we ever get to seeing a heart in action is in the diagrams of medical textbooks. There, for the sake of clarity, everything is colored like a map. When we see a living heart, perhaps during a televised operation, we may be totally confused. It looks a mess. It's hard to relate the beating heart to the textbook diagram. It's difficult to distinguish the various parts. It's even harder to imagine how anyone ever came to understand what was going on in the heart. Galen, who lived in the second century, said the heart was like a lamp burning oily fluid from the liver and sending fumes out through the windpipe. We talk about the heart, not as a lamp, but as a pump and, of course, until pumps were invented, no one could say that about the heart. Once there was a new image, new things could be discovered. Parts of the heart could be understood in terms of parts of the pump.[8]

The close relationship between what we imagine to be there, and what we see to be there, often hides the use of imagination in perception and knowledge. It all seems so obvious when we know what we are looking at. But the way our images and metaphors are embedded in our descriptions of reality means that imagination isn't just a tool that enables us to discover what is really there. What we actually say is really there, is a work of imagination. It needs to be stressed that this is not to say that there is nothing there, that everything is imaginary or that it's all a dream. It is to say that our description of what is there is a work of imagination.

This calls for humility. There may be, for example, more than one way to describe what we see. Harvey's understanding of the heart as a pump succeeded Galen's but in some scientific scenarios, several images of reality may be used at the same time, as with wave and particle theories of light. Also, our understanding of reality is always temporary, always of our time and always likely to be superceded. Just as the imagery of art changes, so does the imagery of understanding and knowledge. Again, this isn't to say that our understanding and knowledge is merely fashionable. It is to say that like art, our knowledge is never final and never absolute.

Our claim that imagination takes us to the heart of God is also seen in the close relationship between morality and imagination.[9] Again the connection is more intimate than we often think. "Imagine what it would be like to be in their shoes," we say in our encouragement to motivate people. John Lennon bids us

> Imagine no possessions,
> I wonder if you can,
> No need for greed or hunger,
> A brotherhood of man,
> Imagine all the people
> Sharing all the world. [10]

But imagination is more than a motivating force for our actions. Much of the time, we think of morality in terms of rules. Rules such as the Ten Commandments, or an update of them, form the basis of how we should behave. Morality is following the rules. And, of course, in general, we do think that it's wrong to steal or to murder. On the whole, we do need some guiding principles. But it is *on the whole* and *in general* that the rules are to be followed. When it comes to the detail of everyday life, then we may have to decide whether a particular killing was murder, self-defense or justifiable homicide. And to do that, we need to rehearse what happened in a variety of ways, with different interpretations of the evidence. And that takes imagination.

Many of the decisions we have to take do not easily fall

under the pattern of our moral rules and codes of behavior. Should we act to prevent our children following a course of action we think to be wrong? Should we turn off the life-support machine? Indeed in the minutiae of life, and the small actions that brought us to our present situation, it's not always obvious that there was even a decision to make. And yet those small steps can have huge consequences. When decisions are hard to codify, we sometimes talk about pursuing certain values. If we do what is loving and just, then we shall be on the right track. Morality is the pursuit of values. But just as it is hard to decide whether a particular killing was murder, self-defense or justifiable homicide, so finding the just course of action for everyone concerned is difficult. Our values, like our rules, don't always yield enough detail to make them practical and don't offer enough guidance when different values conflict with each other. Even when we are confident that our rules and values offer useful guidance, we need imagination to see how they are relevant, and how they apply to our situation.

And then some situations seem to have no precedent. Here all we can do is try to imagine different possibilities. How would we feel about ourselves if we took this course of action? What effects might it have on others? What else might happen as a consequence? What might go wrong? Again we have to use imagination. And it's how we judge our behavior. The prosecution asks us to imagine the accused as having evil intentions, as acting to achieve certain ends, or bringing about unwanted consequences and to interpret the evidence accordingly. The defense asks us to imagine a different scenario.

The vital role of imagination in our ethical life is sharply brought into focus when people talk of the need to be detached, objective and reasonable and to make our decisions in the cold light of day. It implies that the involvement of our emotions and imaginations will cloud our judgment. The clarity of reason and logic will be obscured. But most of us would say that such detached behavior is cold-blooded. We bring imagination to bear because it enables us to see the possibilities that lie within the reality of our situation. To imagine isn't to "imagine things" or drift off into the fanciful, it's to see the full potential of the present.

Imagination, then, is vital in providing the wisdom for our understanding and action. For us as Christians, the connection with the Spirit and Wisdom of God is neatly portrayed in the Book of Proverbs where Wisdom is depicted at the side of God: "playing in his presence, playing on the earth when he had finished it".[11] It is also portrayed in the opening of the fourth Gospel where John uses the expression the Word of God, the *logos* (to use the Greek term).[12] *Logos* means not only the "expression" of God but also the "intelligibility" of God. Creative expression and intelligibility come together, in God, in the Holy Spirit, through Christ, the Word of God.

The coming together of imagination and truth in Christ,

the Word of God, emphasizes the sacrificial work of the Spirit. The cost for an artist pursuing their vision is often considerable. Chopin is said to have agonized over his compositions "weeping, walking, breaking pens, repeating and altering a bar a hundred times". The opposition faced by scientists, perhaps most famously by Galileo, has sometimes been harsh. Social reformers have been persecuted for their attempts to realize their vision for the world. And while this isn't the fate of all artists, scientists and social reformers, when it does occur, it represents the cost of faith and mirrors the vulnerability and suffering of Christ, the Word made Flesh.

Chapter 10

in faith

It used to be thought that gods lived on mountains like Mount Olympus and Mount Sion. From the mountain peaks, gods could see everything and know everything that was happening below. With their homes concealed in the clouds, the gods were invisible and their thoughts hidden from human sight. In volcanic eruptions, they displayed their displeasure with human upstarts who attempted to get above themselves. A mountain spirituality meant that only the youngest, fittest and most courageous pioneers communed with the gods. Only the select few could bear the cost of faith, make the climb, see the gods face to face, gain divine knowledge and the onerous responsibility of passing it on to those below.

This spiritual path to divine knowledge is reflected in our stories. Moses, the prophet of ancient Israel, brings his people to the foot of Mount Sinai.[1] They are warned, on pain of death, to stay well clear of the mountain while he makes the climb to speak with God. In thunder and lightening, fire and earthquake, the divine presence is revealed. The people below are so terrified that they refuse to listen directly to God. Moses is given the divine commandments written on tablets of stone and charged with the responsibility of delivering them to the people.

In another tradition, Plato, in his *Republic*, tells a story of prisoners held, since their birth, in a cave, deep under the earth.[2] One prisoner is selected, released and dragged up to the surface and into the daylight where he sees the awful truth of their situation and imprisonment. The responsibility of telling his fellow prisoners proves too much as he fumbles his way back into the gloomy cave. They taunt him and kill him.

Something of a mountain top spirituality is built into the plan of many churches. Each part of the journey into these churches involves climbing steps: moving from outside to inside the church; moving from the nave, the main body of the church, to the chancel, the area where the choir and priests sit; moving finally into the sanctuary and up to the altar. In Canterbury Cathedral, the altar stands several feet higher than the nave floor. Often, and certainly in worship, only specially designated people, dressed in robes, are allowed into certain areas of the church. There may even be a screen or rail preventing movement from one part of the church to another. Only at special dramatic moments in worship are these boundaries crossed: the priest enters the nave to read the Gospel; the people enter the chancel to take communion.

But not all churches are built in this way, and the differences reflect different understandings of the spiritual path. The Roman Catholic Cathedral in Liverpool, affectionately known as "Paddy's Wigwam", is built "in the round", with the altar at the center of the circle and the congregation sitting round it. Other churches and chapels are dominated by a huge, central pulpit or a baptismal pool. A Friends Meeting House will have no altar, no pulpit, no screened off areas, no special robes. And there are some churches that do not even have a special building in which to meet. Members of a "house church" gather in each other's homes to worship. All these reflect a church's understanding of the spiritual path, the way to God and where authority is to be found.

Architecture has such a strong influence upon faith and its practice that reformations in faith lead to new styles of church and chapel design. Methodism, the Oxford Movement, Vatican II, all had a profound influence upon church architecture, reflecting their different understandings of the priesthood, the authority of the Bible, the sacraments, the importance of mystery and the role of the lay congregation. These designed features and their effects often go unnoticed until a change is brought about. When restoration work was being undertaken on my church, the congregation and I had to worship in the church hall. We used the same service, the same hymns, the same church silver and the same vestments. But people said they enjoyed the experience so much that they would prefer to stay in the church hall! Forget the repairs. Sell the church! This had nothing to with the heat of the building: it was the middle of summer! It had everything to do with the members of the congregation being able to sit closer to each other and to the priest. It had everything to do with the less formal posture that could be adopted in a chair as opposed to a pew. It had everything to do with the colorful children's pictures on the walls. It had everything to do with "being on the same level". It was a new experience of worship.

What is true of architecture is true of every aspect of faith. Churches aren't the only aspect of faith to be designed. And the design is not simply a matter of taste; it's a reflection of the understanding of the path of faith itself. So the re-ordering of churches isn't just giving them a makeover; it's a revision of the spiritual life. Makeover programs on the television encourage us to paint our walls according to the fashion of the moment and increase our sense of space. More ambitious grand designs, however, will have us tear down the walls and re-model our houses to reflect our changing lifestyles and the use we like to make of our space. Separate rooms give way to open-plan living spaces; small kitchens and dining rooms give way to cooking spaces that open out in full view of the dining areas; small toilets and bathrooms give way to greatly enlarged wet rooms - all to reflect the priorities of our contemporary living.

When it comes to faith, we are understandably nervous of admitting all this. Can our understanding of the path of faith really change? Should design play such a large part in the practice of faith? Yet no form of faith, worship or prayer is handed down from God on tablets of stone in unchangeable form. Even the most fundamentalist believer must acknowledge that to some degree at least, faith is a human creation. But for many, a designer faith sounds ominously like social engineering and behavior management. It is one thing to talk about liturgy as drama, quite another to suggest that every aspect of the service and its setting has been designed for maximum impact on the worshippers. Believers are particularly sensitive to accusations of being under the influence of mass hysteria or an opium for the people.

Faith and the church come to birth through the Holy Spirit, through the creative imagination of God. We call Pentecost, the celebration of the coming of the Holy Spirit to the disciples, "the church's birthday". When, in baptism, we are initiated into the community of faith, we are promised the Holy Spirit. In communion, the power of the Holy Spirit enables us to see the bread and wine as the body and blood of Christ, renewing us and inspiring us with the love of God. Christians living in the Spirit will, therefore, expect to be continually recreated. The Spirit pictured as fire will refine and redefine us. The Spirit as wind will transport us in new directions and to new places.

Nowhere should this creative work of the Spirit be more clearly seen than in the church's use of the Bible. The only time most people hear a passage read from the bible is at a wedding, funeral or carol service. For most of the time, and primarily, the reading of the Bible *is* part of the worship of the church community. Of course, the Bible contains historical material and will be of interest to those who want to learn about the history of Israel or the history of the early Church. But, as Christians, this isn't our main use of the Bible. We read it, as a community, for inspiration and guidance and therefore our chief task is to make the scriptures speak to us afresh each time we hear them.

In this sense, the scriptures have to be performed.[3] If we want a great piece of music to give us pleasure, we have to do more than simply play the notes. We have to perform it. To make the text of a Shakespeare play inspire us, we have to do more than simply read the words. We have to perform it in a way that brings it alive and speaks to our condition. It's not a matter of dressing up and acting out the Bible as if it were a play - though there are good examples of that. Rather, it's gathering with the community and asking what this scripture moves us to do. And that will vary each time we read it, and will be the result of imaginatively and collectively making meaning for our lives through the scripture. So that when we read a parable, for example, we are not so much looking at a picture of the Christian life but at a mirror. We look to see how our lives today are reflected in this parable? How is this story a metaphor of our lives? How is this piece of history, our history? And we look for the creative imagination of the Holy Spirit, to guide us.

For Christians, the Holy Spirit takes them one step further, right to the very heart of the mystery of God. Creativity keeps faith alive. Imagination enables the scriptures to speak to us. Design facilitates the Church's coming together. And the Spirit, the wisdom, creativity and imagination of God in us, leads us even to the heart of God. As the Spirit unites us in the Body of Christ so the Spirit unites us with that in which we live and move and have our being.

It may seem utterly blasphemous to relate the Holy Spirit to imagination and say that the imagination takes us into God. It seems as if we were saying that God is a figment of our imaginations; that God is no more real than the fairies, or that God exists only in our imaginations. This is to see the imagination solely as a creative process that *produces* fantastical fictions. Equally it may seem blasphemous because to make an image of God is to make an idol. However this is to see the imagination solely as a perceptive process that *reproduces* images of reality. In fact, as we have seen in Chapter Nine, the imagination is a more complex set of processes. It makes connections, sees things as similar to other things, invents new metaphors and so brings together creativity and truth. We lie back in the bath and let our minds wander; we dream dreams and give our imagination free play. It is then that we are struck with the profoundest perception of reality and leap from the water with a cry of "*Eureka*".

How do we know that our imaginations haven't wandered from the path to truth? How do we know that the truth we have imaginatively perceived is not an illusion? It is a very real danger. Religious delusions lead to the most dangerous fanaticism. In an attempt to be free from delusion, many will try to be rid of imagination altogether. The meaning of the scriptures, they say, is given and unalterable. The path of faith is laid down for all time. But to take imagination out of religion is to take the spirit out of our faith. Literalism in faith is like insisting that a play be performed for all time with the same costumes and stage directions. It robs it of its ability to speak to us. Fundamentalism in religion is like insisting that we all live the same way, wear the same clothes and speak the same language. It denies us of our individuality and robs us of our responsibility. To avoid religious fanaticism we must recognize the symbolic, metaphorical and creative aspects of faith.

To avoid the danger of delusion in faith we need more imagination, not less. Our faith has to be firmly rooted in the creative community of the Spirit. Our understandings have to be tested in that community. They must stand the test of experience and be subject to the wider criticism of the best of all human endeavor. The more all-embracing, accepting and encouraging of greater exploration, the less likely we are to be subject to religious delusion. There are no guarantees. Faith remains a risky business and its participants like all artists will recognize the vulnerability of their endeavor.

Chapter 11

in earth

My granddad was a violin teacher and the organist of Macclesfield Parish Church. When the First World War came, his pupils joined up, many never to return. So he changed his profession and became an engineer. His advice to his son, my father, was not to become a music teacher. It was too risky. I used to be a music teacher and now my daughters are furthering their musical education. What advice do I give them?

Take your cue from Vanessa Mae, I could say. Give "techno synth interpretations of Bach dancing in wet T shirts". You will have no trouble making a living. But heed the warning of the all-woman string quartet *Bond*. Their "bare midriffs and pouting poses" may have catapulted *Bond* to chart success with their debut album, but the music establishment has shown less enthusiasm for the "classical

Spice Girls" than the paying public. The music industry banned them from the classical charts after one week, declaring that Bond's brand of music owed more to "Boyzone than Beethoven".[1]

Away from Classic FM, the Nigel Kennedys and Charlotte Churches, another world of music strives for public attention. In 1999 The Royal Opera House Covent Garden received £75.5m of National Lottery money[2] and was subsidized to the tune of £20m.[3] And yet very, very few people go to the opera. Only about 5% of the population, and only 2% of young people, in the UK ever attend the theatre, the ballet or the opera. A tiny proportion of that 5% ever go to an opera.[4] It makes the Millennium Dome seem like a good deal. Welcome to the world of classical music. Welcome to today's culture.

My younger daughter, as a chorister at Evensong, always insisted on praying in the Lord's Prayer "Thy will be done, in earth as it is in heaven." That's how it reads in the *Book of Common Prayer* but in many churches people have been taught to say "on earth". I'm not quite sure what it says about my daughter that she prefers the printed word but I like the phrase "in earth". It suggests that we don't merely live on earth, as we might one day live on the moon, but remain much more deeply rooted in the earth. So much so that if we make a major move, we have, as we say, to uproot ourselves.

Many of the parables in the New Testament are about seeds being sown in the earth. The better the soil in which they are sown, the stronger the roots and the greater the harvest. Today, when we talk about our growth, our personal growth, we are more likely to talk about culture than agriculture. The soil in which we grow is the fast moving, ever-changing world of culture.

If, as we have said, religious faith is a human creation involving the creative imagination, then religious faith is part of human culture. The world of faith is like the world of culture, like the world of today's classical music. It raises some interesting questions. The church going statistics quoted in Chapter Two may not be impressive but then, what percentage of the population do we expect to attend church as compared to the opera? Do we think of worship as a highbrow activity? Is it high art? Is there a popular religious culture and a Vanessa Mae of the religious world?

The world of faith *is* like the world of culture. We talk about our faith shaping and nourishing our lives. In it we live and move and have our being. Culture is about cultivation and growth and it too is that in which we put down roots and grow. Religion has its roots in a word meaning "to bind". Faith binds its followers together. So does culture. Faith determines how believers behave and respond to those around them. So does culture. Faith looks to spread itself around. The gospel has its evangelists as culture has its colonizers.

Consider, the word culture, once used for most people's everyday work, later took on a capital C and became

Culture, the rather refined expression of a cultivated society. Such highbrow pursuits came under the patronage of the aristocracy while the lower classes had their own, more earthy, low-brow amusements. Today we are more likely to talk about high art versus the popular, mass, consumerist culture. This can become very snobbish and elitist. Here too there are parallels to religion. Some will say there is a common, unreflected, unconscious inheritance of faith, a folk religion of the people, and in addition there is the more theologically articulated faith. Elitism and snobbery aren't far away when people talk of the "person in the pew" with their "simple faith".

For some, all this is largely irrelevant. The world of faith is not, and should not, be part of the world of culture. Faith is an alternative world. *Christian Blue Pages*, the Christian community's equivalent to *Gay to Z*, advertises the services of every kind of Christian business from dentists to driving instructors.[5] So it's possible to live our whole lives in a separate Christian world where our children go to a Christian school, where we shop and deal only with Christian traders and are entertained at Christian clubs listening to Christian music groups. Other faiths have their directories too. There is the *Muslim Directory* and *Sikh Chamber*.[6] Is this the future for faith? Can faith only succeed by building up strong, faith-based counter-cultures?

Faith cannot afford to retreat into its own ghetto. *The Cantle Report, Community Cohesion*, examining disturbances in British towns and cities in the spring and summer of 2001, found a "depth of polarization" centered around segregated communities.

> Separate educational arrangements, community and voluntary bodies, employment, places of worship, language, social and cultural networks, mean that many communities operate on the basis of a series of parallel lives. These lives often do not seem to touch at any point, let alone overlap and promote any meaningful interchanges.[7]

While some try to reject the world of culture for an alternative world of faith, others have given up on the world of faith altogether. For them culture has become their religion. Many of those who have abandoned their religion say that they go for walks, listen to music, read books, go to the theatre or meditate in a relaxing bath surrounded by lighted candles. Their cultural pursuits more than fill the void left by religion. Why worry if faith disappears? Doesn't culture do a better job?

In *The Idea of Culture* Terry Eagleton warns that culture isn't robust enough to become a substitute for religion.[8] Indeed if it tries to take over from religion it begins to portray pathological symptoms. One of these symptoms is the equating of culture solely with the arts. To be cultured is to know about the arts, and the civilized person is the one who patronizes the arts. But if culture is reduced to this narrow view, human creativity is equally restricted. As we have seen in the previous chapters, imagination and creativity play a vital role in our understanding, our morality and, indeed, all human affairs.

Another pathological symptom of culture trying to take over from religion, according to Eagleton, is the loss of moral and political impetus. The civilized and cultured person becomes detached from the world, standing aloof from its messiness. As an example Eagleton points to Matthew Arnold, the writer of "Dover Beach", the poem quoted earlier in Chapter Two. Despite thinking that culture was a form of social improvement, Arnold himself refused to take sides over the slavery question in the American Civil War. Rather than being driven to act against slavery, his interest in culture was an antidote to politics, keeping his mind free from disturbances and any kind of enthusiasm. To be committed is to be uncultivated.

Eagleton therefore argues for a more modest view of culture. The problems we face in the world are to do with war, famine, poverty, disease, debt, drugs, environmental pollution, and the displacement of peoples. While these may be bound up with questions of belief and identity, none of them, he says, are primarily cultural but material, and cultural theorists and practitioners have therefore little to say about their resolution. In trying to assume a political and religious importance culture, he says has grown "immodest and overweening".[9] We see something of this in the saints of modern culture, the celebrities who vie for attention in the tabloid press and on the television. While many are superbly good at practicing their art, be it on stage or screen, when every detail of their lives is revealed in the tabloids, they assume an importance far beyond their achievements.

Religion, must take its place within today's fast-moving and highly diverse world, if it is to continue, if it is to avoid fundamentalism and fanaticism, and if it is not be taken over by culture. It must not retreat into its own ghetto nor allow itself to be taken over. It is one of the most challenging issues facing the faith communities today.

Is this a description of the church of today?

archaic, quaint, thinly attended, and not done as well as it used to be. . . Is all experiment over? Is there no adventure, no ambition, no courage, no politics, no spirituality?[10]

This passage written by Richard Eyre is, in fact, from a lecture about the theatre. He continues:

And the audience has changed. No theatre now can count on a "theatre going constituency". These have vanished in the same way congregations have vanished from churches.

Such an analysis ought to bring some comfort to us in the church. Those who bombard us with the church

statistics quoted in Chapter Two and declare CHURCH
DEAD & BURIED BY 2040 should take heed. The
problems facing the church today are no different and no
worse than those facing many cultural institutions. Political
organizations and voluntary bodies as well as artistic
institutions face the challenges of today's culture.

Ronald Eyre sees three ways of improving access to
the theatre: through education, through touring and
through adequate funding. The church needs to adopt
such strategies to survive. Indeed the churches are
already exploring these avenues. Much effort is put into
evangelistic initiatives such as the *Alpha Course*. The
same effort and resources need to be given to education
regarding all aspects of the church, its worship, history and
teaching, across a broad spectrum of orthodoxy. Some will
argue that the church, like the institutions of high art, is
elitist and excludes many young people. But it's not quite
so simple. Most of the performing arts are dedicated to very
highly skilled and gifted people, and require a certain
amount of concentration and training. That they may
therefore have a limited audience doesn't necessarily mean
that such art is elitist or obscure. Church services also
require a degree of concentration and participation; indeed
the word liturgy means, "work of the people". Great
imagination is needed to fire young people's enthusiasm
for a Shakespeare play. No less thought is needed to fire
people's enthusiasm for one of the churches' liturgies.
A radical faith committed to the Spirit's creative and

imaginative work is well placed to respond to this challenge.

Part of the program of most theatre companies involves touring, with workshops and performances in small-scale venues. Symphony orchestras have similar projects. The church is beginning to move outside the church walls and find ways of "being church", as it says, within community groups. A radical faith, committed to finding the God of life in the whole of life will of necessity move beyond the church walls and community.

Funding is a major issue for many churches in England, but imaginative solutions are being encouraged for the use and maintenance of church buildings and the deployment of ministers. Where these have been introduced the church is liberated to concentrate on providing a vision and a prophetic voice within today's culture. A faith that sees the changing design and use of churches will be eager to find imaginative use for its buildings.

The prophets of doom declare that God is dead. They claim to hear the "melancholy, long, withdrawing roar of the sea of faith", the last gasp of the church soon to be buried in the same grave. They may have mistakenly heard the sound of the returning tide.

Chapter 12
in death

"Earth to earth, ashes to ashes, dust to dust." The *Book of Common Prayer* "Burial Service" makes no bones about the transitory nature of life. "In the midst of life we are in death: of whom may we seek for succour but of thee, O Lord." The process of living is the process of dying.

Everyday from our mid-20s, so we are told, we lose 7000 brain cells a day. It isn't just our bodies that are in a continual state of decay. Our relationships change too. We move house and change jobs and a friendship that was once so strong and supportive dwindles away to a few photographs and a card at Christmas. Even our most loving relationships can come to an end, sometimes a tragic and abrupt end. It's the risk we take with all our loving and befriending. It's a hard lesson to learn. Dying is not something that comes after living. Living and dying are part of the same process.

Death too is part of life. American research indicates that children will have seen as many 250,000 acts of violence and 40,000 attempted murders on television by the time they are 18.[1] But the vast majority of these deaths are simply the elimination of characters. In Britain, where there is a long tradition of murder mysteries, each episode of a popular series like *Midsomer Murders* will clock up a body count of at least half a dozen, making the fictitious English village the most dangerous place on earth![2] Such programs achieve their effect, whether humorous or serious, by limiting the play of our imaginations. We are not encouraged to think too deeply about the pain and suffering caused by these acts of violence. Governments in war employ a similar strategy. Describing casualties as "human collateral damage", they hope to maintain our political support. Perhaps we are happy not to be made to think too deeply while we're being entertained; when it comes to war we have no excuse.

A similar limiting of imagination is seen in talk about heaven. In the hope of bringing comfort to the bereaved, we are encouraged to think of being reunited with our friends and family, and living a life of unending happiness. But we are not encouraged to think too deeply. For if we imagined the full implications of these meetings, and what it might be like to live an unending life, our desire for heaven would drain away. An unending life, in the long run and even in the best of company, would become utterly confusing and boring.[3]

What age shall we be in the "after life"? If we've been married a number of times on earth, who will we be married to in heaven?[4] What purpose will there be in an endless repetition of pleasures? Our reflections run into difficulty because we are asked to think of heaven as the continuing story of our lives, the final chapter in our personal biography. Heaven is not the next chapter of the story of our lives; it's the end of them, their completion and fulfillment. The story comes to an end. There is no more narrative to tell. It is finished.[5]

Just as dying is not a process that occurs after living so in the Christian tradition the eternal life of heaven is not something that occurs after death.[6] Christian orthodoxy does not speak about the immortality of the soul or about the inevitability of the story continuing. Death brings our lives to an end. We are born and we die and any talk of life "after" death is, therefore, necessarily metaphorical. So too the resurrection of Jesus is not seen in Christian theology as the continuing story of Jesus' life. It is his glorification, his vindication, the completion of his work and the salvation of the world. In talking of Jesus' resurrection, it is not what happens to Jesus *after* his death that matters but what is manifest *in* his death.

For Christians, the key phrase for describing our ultimate end is "in God". Our final satisfaction is to lose ourselves in God. Bertrand Russell, although not writing from a Christian conviction, echoes this sense of being lost in the ocean of existence:

> An individual human existence should be like a river - small at first, narrowly confined within its banks, and rushing passionately past boulders and over waterfalls.
> Gradually the river grows wider, the banks recede, the waters flow more quietly, and, in the end, without any visible break, they become merged with the sea.[7]

These words also echo the sense of the story coming to an end in the language of rest. "Our hearts our restless till they find their rest in God" wrote Augustine.[8] The Sabbath rest in the creation story[9] becomes the Christian's fulfillment in God.[10] Our final rest, as indeed our whole life, is in God.

Where is the comfort in this? What hope for us if we are not going to meet our family and friends, or see the lives of those cut short, living on in heaven? Such hopes would be unlikely to compensate for the pain suffered by the dying or the bereaved. While we may imagine the dead called away to greater works in a far off country, the pain of separation will still exist. There is simply no compensation for some tragedies of life.

Rather than look for the continuation of our loved ones' story in heaven, we begin to look for the perfections of their lives that symbolize their life in God. We look for those qualities that, even in a life cut short, were complete and whole. Very often these will be seen through a photograph, a picture or a memory serving as icons of their love, joy, determination and courage.[11] No more poignantly is this seen than on the grave of a very young child. Teddies and toys are placed alongside the flowers at the funeral. Very often these remain for some time to come. But as the months and years go by, there is a recognition that had they lived, the child would now be at school, in their teens and becoming a young adult. Sometimes, as the flowers are changed, there is an attempt to reflect this with new toys appropriate for their imagined age. But in the fullness of time, we begin to realize that the attempt to carry on the story of their lives is a vain attempt to remember them; better the battered teddy, the old photograph and the remembered smile that brings back to us the bundle of fun which brought joy to our lives for that short time. In God, all lives are complete and whole and their perfections become part of the perfection of God.

Our journey through bereavement becomes a journey that has already been traced in this book. Once again we are taken away from heaven down to earth. We follow the journey of Christ into our humanity. We abandon pictures of lives continuing in heaven for lives lived on earth. In biblical jargon we look for the kingdom of heaven on earth.

The phrase "kingdom of heaven" is found in Matthew's Gospel but it is interchangeable with the phrase "kingdom of God" used in other gospels and the rest of the New Testament. The gospel writers use the phrase to sum up Jesus' whole mission. He describes his purpose as preaching the kingdom of God.[12] The phrase occurs in some fifty sayings in the gospels. Sometimes Jesus suggests that the kingdom is already in the midst of his hearers;[13] sometimes it is an event about to happen.[14] The interpretation of the phrase by New Testament scholars has been very diverse. But the most striking feature of Jesus' teaching is that it is anything but dogmatic. Jesus does not present a systematic set of doctrines. He tells parables and stories and acts in thought-provoking ways. His sayings and his life are icons for our contemplation and prayer, enabling us to discover the presence of God wherever we are now, motivating us to work for greater justice and peace and bring heaven down to earth.

In speaking of the kingdom both as a present and future fulfillment, the kingdom sayings reflect the central issue of God's omnipresence, God's relationship to time and place. God, according to the tradition, is limited neither by time nor by space. God is timeless and any attempt to talk about the relationship of God to time will be in metaphor. But as is clear from our explorations from the mystery of life to the mystery of death, all talk about God is metaphorical. If Christians have sometimes been slow to make this clear, and been guilty of gross literalism, so too have those who have opposed them.

Yet the argument is made that by insisting on the

metaphorical nature of religious language we rob it of any meaning. As Christians however, the meaning of our talk about God emerges in three ways.

First, by insisting on the limitations of our talk about God, we focus attention on the real mysteries of life. The mystery of God is manifest not in another unseen place and time but in the mysteries of life itself, in the mystery of its very being, its determined and indeterminate nature, in the mystery of personhood and love, in the mystery of imagination and death. In all these, believers find themselves in the mystery of God. The Christian focus is not on the question of the reality of the existence of God. Indeed God is often spoken of as the one whose existence is not in doubt.[15] Rather attention is turned to the nature, mystery and paradox of life in which the mystery of God is revealed.

Secondly, by emphasizing the limitations and metaphorical nature of all talk about God, we seek to turn our attention away from what can be said to what can be done. Given the gift of life, personhood and imagination, we seek to live life the full. And when confronted with the meaninglessness of so much suffering and inhuman action, we do not seek to give it meaning. Those who find themselves in the midst of such suffering are not in need of our explanations but our action.

Thirdly, emphasizing the metaphorical nature of religious language changes the character of belief itself. Believing in God is not ticking off a checklist of propositions about the supernatural. God is not the object of our speculation but that in which we live and move and have our being. In God, we make our life. In the mystery of life, personhood and imagination, we work to make a happier and healthier world.

In his novel *Now I Know*, Aidan Chambers offers a definition of belief. He separates the word into "be" and "lief".[16] "Be" is to exist, to live, to have a presence in reality. "Lief" relates to an Old English word for love and means gladly and willingly.

So belief means your will to give all your attention to living with loving gladness in the world you think really does exist.

It sums up the theme of this book. We live gladly and lovingly in the ever-present reality of the mystery of life, personhood and imagination. We believe in God.

Notes

Chapter 1: In

1 Information about the Sea of Faith Network can be found on their website at www.sofn.org.uk

2 For example Lloyd Geering, *Christianity without God* (2002, reprinted Polebridge Press).

Chapter 2: In the bathroom

1 Contemporary Lavender from the Bath House, The Grain Store, Busk Lane, Sedbergh, Cumbria LA10 5HF.

2 Acts of the Apostles 2:3

3 Psalm 133:2

4 Luke 7:37

5 Joanne Harris, *Chocolat* (Black Swan, 1999)

6 Metro Digest, Monday 17th April 2000 page 6

7 Matthew Arnold, *Poetry and Prose*, ed. J. Bryson (London 1967) pp. 144 - 5

8 M.D. Gibson (ed.), *Horae Semiticae X* (Cambridge: Cambridge University, 1913), p. 40.

9 Acts 17:28

Chapter 3: In God

1 See for example Thomas Aquinas, *Summa Contra Gentiles* 2, chapter 15

Chapter 4: In life

1 See Don Cupitt, *The New Religion of Life in Everyday Speech.* (London: SCM Press, 1999) and *Life, Life* (Polebridge Press, 2003)

2 Philippians 3:19

3 See, for example, Acts 9:2, 19: 23, 22:4 and 24:14, 22

4 For a discussion of this see Nicholas Lash, *Believing Three Ways in One God, A Reading of the Apostles' Creed* (SCM Press 1992), pp19 - 21

5 Augustine, *Commentary on John*, xxix, translated by Nicholas Lash op. cit. p20

Chapter 5: In luck

1 Acts 1:15 - 26

2 Jonah 1: 4 - 10

3 Luke 10: 30 - 37

4 This and other aspects of the parables are explored at length in D.M. Mackinnon, *The Problem of Metaphysics* (Cambridge

University Press, 1974), chapter 12

5 Job 1

6 Matthew 5: 45

7 John 9: 2

Chapter 6: In Christ

1 Colossians 1:2, Phillipians 1:1

2 Romans 6:3, Galatians 3:27

3 2 Corinthians 5:17

4 I Corinthians 15:22

5 Galatians 2: 20

6 Galatians 3: 28

7 Romans 12: 5, 1 Corinthians 12: 27

8 Michael Goulder in *Midrash and Lection in Matthew* (London, SPCK 1974) and *The Evangelists' Calendar, A Lectionary Explanation of the Development of Scripture* (London, SPCK 1978) explores this idea in great detail.

9 Philippians 2: 4 - 8

10 Mark 11: 1 - 10

11 John 13: 1 - 11

Chapter 7: In person

1 E.g. Matthew 3: 17, Galatians 2: 20

2 From the Nicene Creed.

3 Psalm 139: 7 - 12

4 Augustine, *Soliliques*

Chapter 8: In love

1 For a long an interesting discussion of this question see John D. Caputo, *On Religion*, (Routledge 2001)

2 This argument is explored in great detail in Gareth Moore, *Believing in God* (T & T Clark 1988), chapter 4

3 1 John 4: 20

4 Luke 15: 8 - 10

5 Luke 15: 11 - 32

6 1 John 4: 18

7 Matthew 10: 28 see again Gareth Moore *op.cit.*

8 Matthew 10: 31 - 32

Chapter 9: In spirit

1 It is interesting that the increasing number of books concentrating on the Holy Spirit is matched by those on the imagination. On the place of imagination within religion see, for example, Paul Avis *God and the Creative Imagination* (London, 1999), Garrett Green *Imagining God:*

Theology and the Religious imagination (Grand Rapids, 1999), Gordon Kaufman *The Theological Imagination: Constructing the Concept of God* (Philadelphia, 1981)

2　Genesis 1: 2

3　E.g. Isaiah 11: 2, Ephesians 1: 17

4　Joel 2: 28

5　Galatians 5: 22

6　Colossians 3: 14

7　John Macintyre, speaking at the Edinburgh Festival on art of religion, spoke of Pentecost as, "wholehearted expression of the almost unlimited imagination of God."

8　See Jonathan Miller, *The Body in Question* (Jonathan Cape 1978) chapter 5

9　This topic can be explored through, for example, e.g. Mark Johnson, *Moral Imagination: Implication of Cognitive Science for Eithics* (Chicago: university of Chicago Press, 1933); Mary Warnock, *Imagination* (University of California Press, 1976), *Imagination and Time* (Blackwell, 1994), Patricia Werhane, *Moral Imagination and Management Decision-Making* (Oxford University Press, 1999)

10　From *Imagine* by John Lennon 1971

11　Proverbs 8: 30

12　John 1

Chapter 10: In faith

1　Exodus 19

2　Plato, *The Republic* Book VII

3　See, for example, Stephen Barton's *Invitation to the Scriptures* (SPCK 1997) p.116 ff

Chapter 11: In earth

1　*The Guardian* 16th October, 2000

2　National Audit Office Press Office Notice, 14th May 1999

3　Arts Council subsidy for 2000 / 2001

4　Figures can be found in the *General Household Survey* published annually by the National Statistics Office

5　Their website is www.christianbluepages.com

6　www.muslimdirectory.co.uk and www.sikhchamber.com

7　*Community Cohesion: A Report of the Independent Review Team* (Home Office 2001) p.10 2.1

8　Terry Eagleton, *The Idea of Culture*

(Blackwell 2000)

9　*Op. cit* p. 131

10　This is the beginning of a lecture to the Royal Institute (*The Guardian* 25th March 2000) by Richard Eyre in which he says the theatre is "often regarded in Britain as the cricket of the performing arts".

Chapter 12: In death

1　Lovinger, Robert "Culture shock: Too much violence?" Internet. 20 Sept. 1998.

2　*Midsomer Murders* first broadcast in 1997, won for its producers 'Bentley Productions' the best drama award for that year. Based on the Inspector Barnaby Books by Caroline Graham, it averages 8 million viewers in the UK.

3　For a discussion of this see Bernard Williams "The Makropulos Case; reflec tions on the tedium of immortality" in *Problems of the Self* (Cambridge University Press 1973).

4　See Mark 12. 18ff

5　An interesting and detailed discussion of this point can be found in Paul J Griffiths "Nirvana as the Last Thing? The iconic end of the narrative imagination" in *Modern Theology* 16: January 2000

6　For a detailed exploration of the metaphors of eternity and the finality of death in various Christian theologians, see Nicholas Lash, *Theology on Dover Beach* (London: Darton, Longman and Todd, 1979) Chapter 11 "Eternal Life: Life 'after' death".

7　Bertrand Russell *How to Grow Old from Portraits from memory: and other essays,* (London: Reader's Union, 1958)

8　Augustine Confessions Book 1.1

9　Genesis 2. 2, Psalm 95. 7

10　Matthew 11. 29, 1 John 3.19

11　Again, see the discussion of this in Paul J Griffiths *op. cit.*

12　See for example Luke 4.43 and Matthew 4.23 and cf Acts 8.12

13　E.g. Matthew 4.17, Matthew 12.28

14　E.g. Luke 22.22, Matthew 25.31

15　See, for example, Anselm of Canterbury, *Proslogion* (London: SCM Press, 1974) Chapter 3 "God cannot be thought not to exist" edited and translated by Jasper Hopkins and Herbert W. Richardson,

16　Aidan Chambers, *Now I Know*, (Harper Collins, 1987) reprinted Red Fox Definitions pbk., 2000

O

is a symbol of the world,
of oneness and unity. O Books
explores the many paths of wholeness
and spiritual understanding which
different traditions have developed down
the ages. It aims to bring this knowledge
in accessible form, to a general readership,
providing practical spirituality to today's seekers.

For the full list of over 200 titles covering:

- CHILDREN'S PRAYER, NOVELTY AND GIFT BOOKS
- CHILDREN'S CHRISTIAN AND SPIRITUALITY
- CHRISTMAS AND EASTER
- RELIGION/PHILOSOPHY
- SCHOOL TITLES
- ANGELS/CHANNELLING
- HEALING/MEDITATION
- SELF-HELP/RELATIONSHIPS
- ASTROLOGY/NUMEROLOGY
- SPIRITUAL ENQUIRY
- CHRISTIANITY, EVANGELICAL
  AND LIBERAL/RADICAL
- CURRENT AFFAIRS
- HISTORY/BIOGRAPHY
- INSPIRATIONAL/DEVOTIONAL
- WORLD RELIGIONS/INTERFAITH
- BIOGRAPHY AND FICTION
- BIBLE AND REFERENCE
- SCIENCE/PSYCHOLOGY

Please visit our website,
www.O-books.net

The Thoughtful Guide to Faith
Tony Windross

This book is for anyone who would like to take faith seriously but finds their intelligence getting in the way. It outlines, in 37 short chapters, many of the objections raised to formal Christian religion, and suggests ways of dealing with them which do not compromise people's intellectual integrity.

The claim made here is that Christianity is far more about the way we live than the way we think, that faith can work for all of us, and that what we may or may not believe must never be allowed to get in the way of faith.

"A *bombe surprise*, unexpectedly lively, adventurous and radical."
Don Cupitt, Emmanuel College, Cambridge

Tony Windross is an Anglican minister in Norfolk, England, with degrees from Cambridge University.

1-903816-68-8
£9.99 $14.95

The Thoughtful Guide to the Bible
Roy Robinson

Most Christians are unaware of the revolution in how the Bible may be understood that has taken place over the last two hundred years. This book seeks to share the fruits of the Biblical revolution in an easily accessible manner. It seeks to inform you of its main features and to encourage you to do your own thinking and come to your own conclusions.

Roy Robinson is a United Reformed Church minister, now retired and living in England. A former missionary in Zaire this work arises from a lifetime of study and Bible teaching at the Oxted Christian Centre, which he founded.

1-903816-75-0
£14.99 $19.95

The Trouble With God
Building the Republic of Heaven
David Boulton

Millions of people living in the so-called "Christian West" long for a thoroughly modern, intellectually defensible, emotionally satisfying faith which will be unashamedly religious and spiritual in its commitment, but frankly secular in its relevance to this world and this age. Of such is the republic of heaven.

A wonderful repository of religious understanding and a liberal theologian's delight. Modern Believing

Written with clarity and sensitivity, The Trouble With God *will make sense to a lot of people who might describe themselves as lapsed atheists, doubtful about Christian doctrine but believing that there must*

be more to life than a purely materialist journey concerned solely with survival, sufficiency and self-aggrandisement. I recommend it to all.
Tony Benn, former Cabinet minister

The great thing about this book is that it is exactly like its author: it is affectionate, sane, learned and extremely funny. The next best thing to taking David Boulton home for the weekend is to buy it.
Richard Holloway, former Bishop of Edinburgh

David Boulton is a highly entertaining writer, with a great gift of being funny and serious at once. You'll love it!
Don Cupitt, Fellow, Emmanuel College, Cambridge

David Boulton's new book fascinatingly shows how a radical perspective on religion can bring together the religious and the humanist...An engaged and cogent expression of the human/divine vision in modern thought.
David Hart, Westar Fellow

Disarmingly honest and beautifully written...spurring us on to new visions of the future.
Lloyd Geering, author of *Tomorrow's God*

David Boulton, humanist and Quaker, is a former TV producer, writes for many religious and humanist publications, and is a member of the British Government's Broadcasting Standard's Commission.

1 905047 06 1
£11.99 $24.95

Tomorrow's Christian
Adrian B. Smith

What are the sources of true Christianity? Tradition or Scripture? Experience? How far should our interpretation accommodate modern knowledge?

Some take refuge in fundamentalism, others in emotion, many are leaving the Church. But there are others, called here "tomorrow's Christian", who struggle to bring together in a meaningful way traditional Christianity and a contemporary, nourishing understanding and expression of it.

36 short chapters sum up the characteristics of tomorrow's Christian. One who is questioning, ecologically aware, global, evolving, non-theistic, balanced, right-brain, scriptural, prophetic, peace-making, forgiving, empowered, Jesus-following, seeking, free, discerning, post-modernist, meditating, mystical and others. Ideal for discussion groups, and all individuals looking outside their churches for a way to live as Christians.

An inspiring and multi-faceted vision of "tomorrow's Christian." The layout with many short chapters makes the book easy to read and digest. I enjoyed reading this book immensely. I find it stimulating and encouraging.
Philip Sheppard, *Christians Awakening to a New Awareness*

Adrian B. Smith was ordained as a Roman Catholic priest in 1955.

1 903816 97 1
£9.99/$15.95

Good As New
A radical re-telling of the Christian Scriptures
John Henson

This radical new translation conveys the early Christian scriptures in the idiom of today. It is "inclusive," following the principles which Jesus adopted in relation to his culture. It is women, gay and sinner friendly. It follows principles of cultural and contextual translation. It also returns to the selection of books that modern scholarship now agrees were held in most esteem by the early Church.

A presentation of extraordinary power.
Rowan Williams, Archbishop of Canterbury

I can't rate this version of the Christian scriptures highly enough. It is amazingly fresh, imaginative, engaging and bold.
Adrian Thatcher, Professor of Applied Theology, College of St Mark and St John, Plymouth

I found this a literally shocking read. It made me think, it made me laugh, it made me cry, it made me angry and it made me joyful. It made me feel like an early Christian hearing these texts for the first time.
Elizabeth Stuart, Professor of Christian Theology, King Alfred's College, Winchester

It spoke to me with a powerful relevancy that challenged me to re-think all the things that I have been taught.
Tony Campolo, Professor Emeritus of Sociology, Eastern University

With an extraordinary vigour and immediacy, Good As New *constantly challenges, surprises and delights you. Over and over again you feel like you're reading about Jesus for the first time.* Ship of Fools

John Henson, a retired evangelical Baptist minister, has co-ordinated this translation over the last 12 years on behalf of *ONE for Christian Exploration,* a network of radical Christians and over twenty organisations in the UK

1-903816-74-2
£19.99 $29.95 hb
1-90504711-8
£11.99 $19.95 pb

Bringing God Back to Earth
John Hunt

Religion is an essential part of our humanity. We all follow some form of religion, in the original meaning of the word. But organised religion establishes definitions, boundaries and hierarchies which the founders would be amazed by. If we could recover the original teachings and live by them, we could change ourselves and the world for the better. We could bring God back to earth.

"The best modern religious book I have read. A masterwork."
Robert Van de Weyer, author of *A World Religions Bible*

"Answers all the questions you ever wanted to ask about God and some you never even thought of." **Richard Holloway**, former Primus Episcopus and author of *Doubts and Loves*

John Hunt runs a publishing company of which O Books is an imprint.

1-903816-81-5
£9.99 $14.95

The Fall
The Evidence of a Golden Age, 6,000 Years of Insanity and the Dawning of a New Era
Steve Taylor

The Fall is a major work that overturns mainstream current thinking on the nature of civilization and human nature. It draws on the increasing evidence accumulated over recent decades that pre-literate humanity was relatively peaceful and egalitarian, rather than war-like and crude. It is not "natural" for human beings to kill each other, for men to oppress women, for individuals to accumulate massive wealth and power, or to abuse nature. The worldwide myths of a Golden Age or an original paradise have a factual, archaeological basis.

Taylor's ideas are provocative, and never fail to captivate the reader. It is my fervent wish that this important book will have a wide audience and reach the individuals and institutions that mould public opinion and behaviour. In a world where the very existence of humanity is threatened, Steve Taylor offers a visionary yet practical path out of the morass that distorts human nature.
Dr Stanley Krippner, Professor of Psychology, Saybrooke Graduate School, California.

The Fall *is an astonishing work, full of amazing erudition, all brilliantly organised and argued. The argument that human beings have not always been - and do not have to be - such a psychological mess is presented with a beautiful inevitability and logic. The book is a remarkable feat.* **Colin Wilson**

The Fall *is a fascinating heretical work which demonstrates that the myth of the golden age reflects an archaic social reality. Read it and be cured.* **Richard Rudgley**, author of *Lost Civilizations of the Stone Age*

A fascinating, enlightening and inspiring investigation into the roots of human consciousness and a much needed proscription for a truly human future. **Gary Lachmann**, author of *A Secret History of Consciousness*

A thought-provoking diagnosis of the causes of warfare, patriarchy and materialism which holds potential for bringing humans more in harmony with each other, nature, and themselves. **Tim Kasser**, author of *The High Price of Materialism*

Well-argued, thoughtful, provocative and a pleasure to read. **Christopher Ryan**, Institute of Advanced Medicine and Advanced Behavioral Technology, Juarez, Mexico

Steve Taylor is a university and college lecturer in Manchester, England, and spent seven years researching and writing this book. He has written many articles and essays on psychology and spirituality for mainstream magazines and academic journals.

1 905047 20 7
£12.99 $24.95